UNDERSTANDING MONEY INTELLIGENCE

CHALLENGE.PROVOCATION.ADVICE

CRYFORD MUMBA

(MBA,B.A. Econ., Adv. Dip. Proj. Mgt., Dip. Banking, Dip. Marketing, ACCA Finalist, Msc. Finance student)

Trafford rev. 05/17/2011

 www.trafford.com

North America & international
toll-free: 1 888 232 4444 (USA & Canada)
phone: 250 383 6864 ♦ fax: 812 355 4082

CONTENTS

ABOUT THE AUTHOR

Mr. Cryford Mumba read Economics at The University of Zambia and graduated with Bachelor of Arts Degree. He complemented his Economics degree with the Advanced Diploma in Project Management(UK), Diploma in Banking and Financial Services(Zambia), Diploma in Marketing(UK). He then expanded his knowledge of business through the accountancy of ACCA for which he is a finalist. He holds an MBA(RSA) with a thesis "Limited Access to Credit Among Women Market Traders".

Mr. Mumba is the Proprietor and Chief Executive Officer of Premier College of Banking and Finance Limited, a firm specializing in financial training and consulting. His specialist teaching areas include Financial Mathematics, Statistical Analysis, Corporate Finance, Financial Reporting and Economics. He has written extensively on Banking and Finance course. He is the author Understanding Financial Mathematics, Understanding Statistical Analysis and a host of other Banking and Financial Services training manuals. He is also the Editor of The Student Banker Magazine and a columnist on financial matters for Business Analysis Newspaper.

He resides in Lusaka, married and is a supporter of Arsenal Football Club.

PREFACE

There are a few observations that may help the reader through the pages ahead. The data on which this book is based is distilled into ten chapters which form the core tenets of managing money wisely. Some readers may say that these headings are motherhoods, but that's not true. Each chapter in and of itself may seem a platitude, but the intensity of the way in which excellent money managers execute them is as rare as an eclipse of the moon. Further, though some business ideas have been presented in some sections of the book, there has been a limit as to how far I could expound this area because this is not a 'business book' but a 'money book' of which money can come from different sources.

To get the most of the book, I recommend that you go through the chapters in the exact manner they are organized. This is because each chapter is exceptional and is a guidepost to the next chapter. This is regardless of your comfort because each chapter will challenge, provoke and advise you-triple benchmark-which I have used to good effect to my banking students as a lecturer.

- Challenge - The book will challenge the manner you have been managing your money until now. When strongly challenged, do not think of giving me a 'red card' because am inherently immune from it. Just take note!

- Provocation - This book will provoke you to thing and think deeply on your personal circumstances, to correctly understand your strengths and weaknesses with regards to how you manage your money.

- Advice - This book will also advise you on best practice. This is what has been proven to work for individuals committed to wise money management. The advice given can be accepted or rejected and the choice is entirely yours to make. After all, a person who accepts advice is still the one who makes decisions.

The book provides a learning experience that combines admonition with practical illustrative examples. The book prides itself on making the seminars practical and responsive to the reader's needs and emphasizes individual action plan development, and useful quotations to motivate you. This approach ensures an experience that you will find rewarding and technically useful in your individual capacities whatever your station in life.

The book is a special offer to any individual who wants to improve his/her skills and abilities in managing money wisely and achieve life fulfillment. It is directed at individuals whether they own conglomerates, small businesses, salaried employees, politicians, church members, farmers, street vendors, marketeers, students, retirees and any body who has a sense of money.

A book like this is not only a product of current research and colleagues. My predisposition is a product of lifetime. In that vein, I owe special thanks to my mother, Janet Mumba, who shaped my early notions of excellence, and my late father, Nelson Mumba, (RIP) who taught me the values of initiative and enterprising spirit through personal example. Finally, but not the least 'hat off' to my wife -Nivea - for her unwavering support to the project.

Cryford Mumba

Lusaka, Zambia

CHAPTER 1

FINANCIAL RELATIONSHIP- WHAT IS YOUR RELATIONSHIP WITH MONEY

OBJECTIVES

When you finish this chapter, you will have:

- Revealed your subconscious feelings about money
- Analyzed how wisely you manage your money

Sophocles, the ancient Greek playwright, had a very strong opinion of the role of money. As he saw it, "of all evils upon the earth, the worst is money. It is money that sacks cities, and drives men forth from hearth and home; warps and seduces native intelligence, and breeds a habit of dishonesty."

In modern times, people are still seduced by the lure of money and fashion their lives around its pursuit. Money bewitches people. They fret for it, and they sweat for it. They devise most ingenious ways to get it, and most ingenious ways to get rid of it. Money is the only commodity that is good for nothing but to be gotten rid of. It will not feed you, cloth you, shelter you, or amuse you unless you spend it or invest it. It imparts value only in parting. People will almost do anything for money, and money will do almost anything for people. Money is a captivating, circulating, masquerading puzzle.

REVEAL YOUR SUBCONSCIOUS FEELINGS ABOUT MONEY

1. Find a quit place where you can work undisturbed for ten minutes.

2. On the following list of twenty words, to the right of each

word, jot down an abstract symbol that signifies what feelings the word evokes for you. Use lines, circles, spirals, arrows and the like.

3. If you hesitate on a word, indicate that with a tick to the left of the word. Take a moment to think of a symbol. If no ideas come to you, move on.

1. Money		11. Frustration
2. Impulse buying		12. Budget
3. Business		13. Commitment
4. Creditors		14. Decision
5. Sickness		15. Borrowing
6. Bills		16. Myself
7. Assertive		17. Family
8. Interruptions		18. Church
9. Salary		19. Envy
10. Profit		20. Perfect

When you have completed the money symbols test, connect similar symbols with a line. Work with one shape at a time. For example, ◯ for money, ∿⌒ for perfect, √ for assertive, Ξ for budget, and so on can be used. A big circle for money would mean an expanded sense of money in which you believe anything is possible. (Note: there is no correct or incorrect symbol here, it all depends on your feeling with the word).

FINANCIAL MISMANAGEMENT CASE STUDIES

Having completed the money symbols test, proceed to read the following factual cases and identify the involved persons' relationship with money.

CASE STUDY 1

Growing up in a village setting, I was appalled by the behavior of some of the near-by farm laborers at a farm called Mubuyu farms owned by the Lublinkhof family from Holland. During the month these laborers would borrow through a credit scheme locally called 'kaloba' from an unlicensed money- lenders; would drink beers on credit, smoke tobacco locally called 'balani' on credit and all other sorts of credit arrangements. On the payday at the end of the month, his name would be called by the cashier, while his lenders are just on the sides and immediately he leaves the podium they confiscate his pay envelope. Each money lender picks what is due to him and surrenders the envelope to the next money lender and some lenders even receive nothing. The salary was not enough to pay them all. The laborer was poorer on the payday than ever before because on ordinary days, lenders are available to bail him out. A day later he would start the same borrowing fashion creating a cycle of indebtedness.

Further, on the payday at the farm which was heavily publicized, even people from Lusaka selling second hand clothes called 'salaula' knew the exact day (no wonder some robbers robbed the cashiers of K 30 million in late 1990s), there used to be a big game for men-gambling- which is playing cards for money locally known as 'kuuma njuka' in Tonga. Some laborers, would immediately upon being paid head to the game venue, where the game was played for three days and nights continuously. The fortunate ones would add to their salaries by winning but the majority would go home empty-handed. Some would sell their bicycles, shoes, shirts, and other assets at home to continue with the game. Rumor has it that in olden days, even wives at home were pledged!

CASE STUDY 2

As a young man I learnt a lot from my late father's business undertaking. He was the only one who owned and operated a retail shop in Hapwaya village of chief Naluama's area in the 1980s. He was dealing in groceries. As far as village standards were concerned, he was the richest man with cattle, goats, chickens, dogs, bags of maize for sale, full storage barns of maize for consumption and four wives to his name. He taught me to make orders from Lakhi Enterprises and National Wholesalers in Mazabuka and sometimes in Kafue and Lusaka. The business was booming especially at the month-end when nearby farm laborers got paid. The same applied during harvest time when we could barter groceries for maize at a slightly higher price than cash price. This tonnage and tonnage of maize would then be sold to NAMBOARD.

I started selling in his shop at a very tender age. I could also participate in pricing decisions. He used to book or hire vans to transport groceries to his shop but never bothered to buy one for himself. One white man offered him a land rover once but he declined the offer after consulting other people who advised him otherwise. Truly and wrongly he accepted the advice. Towards the end of his life, he died a poor man with the shop no longer functional, one cow, four wives and twenty eight children. Time came when he could not manage to provide a few kwachas for grinding meal, let alone pay school fees for his children. Only two out of twenty eight children completed grade 12! During his hay days, he did not bother to open a bank account just like the late South African Diva Brenda Fasie who is reported never to have had one for whatever reason.

CASE STUDY 3

Another interesting money management case is found in my lecturing career. I lectured at Lusaka Institute for Business Studies, International Tutorial College and Sedter Business Executive College. The owners of these colleges had somewhat interesting relationship with their money.

At Lusaka Institute of Business Studies, the owner a Mr. Daka enjoyed spectacular enrolments for his business courses. There was an accounts clerk named Mr. Mumba who could receive tuition fees from students and deposit them into the college account. Mr. Daka as the only signatory to the account would go and withdraw cash for beer drinking and to appease ladies. Rumor has it that he even bought a house for one of his concubines in garden compound. Money was spent lavishly and debts for various supplies including rentals were on the increase. The man even diverted examination fees to the Institute of Commercial Management (ICM) paid by the students. ICM reported the matter to the local authority (TEVETA) which acted by closing the college! Lecturers were ever owed salaries.

The story is almost the same for International Tutorial College (ITC) owed by a Mr. Lukomona. He misapplied examination fees to Cambridge University for A-level examinations. Business was really booming and the college even attracted minister's sons. That was the end of the once famous A-level training college and the owner ended up in police cells.

At Sedter Business Executive College, I was employed as the college principal. The college was owed by a Mr. Mwale. Among my other duties, I was charged with the responsibility of ensuring the students paid their fees as per terms and conditions but not how it was spent once received. The consultancy division would make a profit margin from a workshop of up to 75% but bills for workshop venue could not be paid as and when they fell due. Accruals on rental and salaries were pilling up like iceberg when temperatures are negative 100°c. At the month-end when the salaries and other bills approximated to be around K11 million were to be settled, there used to be less than K300 000 in the college account.

Meanwhile, during the month in question we would have collected over K20 million in college fees. Where this money went I did not know.

Once I took trouble to ask the accounts clerk as to what happened to collected money. He told me that the owner either withdrew or instructed him to withdraw on his behalf at will. When he hesitated, he used to be told off "this is my company and do as you are told."

Pressure was always on me from lecturers for their accrued salaries and go slow was always eminent.

At a strategic planning workshop in 2005 at Barn Motel, I demanded to be given full responsibility for the college budget. My request received deaf ears and financial difficulties skyrocketed thereafter until I tendered my resignation letter. However, before I could finally leave, bailiffs pounced for the unpaid rental arrears and that was the end of the college.

STUDY CASE 4

My research has revealed glaring results regarding people's incomes and expenditures. The 'traffic officers' as I call them those who wash our cars and 'sell packing spaces' at my work place on Cairo road go home with not less than K60 000 per day. This translates into K1.8 million per month for which they pay no tax. This amount is far much greater than what some senior civil servants earn monthly after deducting pay-as- you- earn (PAYE).The 'traffic officers' largely spend their day's takings on beers and colleagues with the hope that tomorrow is another day to make more. Interesting enough, every morning they are utterly broke. Asked how much they made monthly, their common response is that they have no idea and do not bother. How much do they spend monthly, they say they don't know except the fact that they are able to trace rental expenses!

Keeping the money symbols test and four illustrative cases given above, you can now proceed to fill in the following questionnaire to analyze how wise you manage your money.

Which area of excellent money management was lacking in each of the above case studies? If you cannot pinpoint it right away, don't despair; you will discover the answers as you read the next chapters of this book!

HOW WISELY DO YOU MANAGE YOUR MONEY?

		Often	sometimes	Rarely
1.	Do you prepare regular budgets?	-	-	-
2.	Do you priotise your expenditure according to which items have the highest pay off for you?	-	-	-
3.	Do you overshoot your expenditure regularly?	-	-	-
4.	Do you keep money aside for emergency?	-	-	-
5.	Do you make the best use of your money?	-	-	-
6.	Do you meet your regular expense with some cash to spare?	-	-	-
7.	Do you earn your money morally and/or legally?	-	-	-
8.	Do people know the right time to make cash demands on you?	-	-	-
9.	Do you feel satisfied with your income?	-	-	-
10.	Can you relax during the month without worrying about money?	-	-	-
11.	Can others carry out most of your responsibilities to earn income If you are unable to work for various reasons?	-	-	-
12.	Does your heart bump when you see a bunch of cash?	-	-	-
13.	Do you borrow money?	-	-	-
14.	Do you pay back borrowed money as agreed?	-	-	-
15.	Do you have a bank account?	-	-	-
16.	Does having a cheque book lead you to overspending?	-	-	-
17.	Do you classify your expenditures into high payoffs and low pay offs?	-	-	-
18.	Do you steal money to meet ends?	-	-	-
19.	Do you invest surplus cash?	-	-	-
20.	Do you do something everyday that moves you closer to Your long-range goals?	-	-	-

YOUR SCORES

Give yourself 5 points for every *'often'* you ticked. Give yourself 2 points for every *'sometimes'*. Give yourself 0 points for every *'rarely'*. Add your points together and compare with the scale below:

80-100: you manage your money very well. You are in control of most situations.

61-80: you manage your money well some of the time. However, you need to be more consistent with the money saving strategies you are using.

41-60: you are slipping. Don't let circumstances get the better of you. Apply techniques in this book right way.

21-40: you are loosing control. You are probably too disorganized to enjoy any quality time. Implement the ideas in this book today!

0-20: You are overwhelmed, scattered, frustrated, and most likely under a lot of stress right now. Immediately put into practice the techniques in this book. Every week review the chapters that deal with your problem areas until you begin to see the light.

YOUR FINANCIAL RELATIONSHIP ACTION PLAN

A. Now that you are more than aware of your money management challenges, make a list of the problem areas you want to change.

1.

2.

3.

4.

5.

B. We can't really manage our money until we learn to manage ourselves, much bad money management is the result of bad habits we've developed through the years. Read the next chapter now to break those patterns that work against you.

QUOTES TO CONSIDER

1. Bizarro -True, money can't buy happiness, but it isn't happiness I want. Its money I want.

2. Aesop (550 BC)-The gods help them that help themselves.

3. Abraham Lincoln- Always bear in mind that your resolution to succeed is more important than any other.

4. Woody Allen (1935)-Its not that I'm afraid to die, I just don't want to be there when it happens.

5. Swedish proverb-In spring no one thinks of the snow that fell last year.

CHAPTER 2

FINANCIAL HABITS - HOW TO MAKE A HABIT OF EXCELLENT MONEY INTELLIGENCE

OBJECTIVES

When you finish this chapter, you will be able to:

- Discuss the nature of financial habits

- Breakout of self-made ruts.

- Kick self defeating habits

- Follow your own personalized habit control action plan

Resolutions, as we all know, are easy to make- and easy to break. Not so with habits: they are pretty difficult. As you read this book, you will learn enough new techniques to make you an expert on money intelligence. But how can you avoid slipping back into all those old, discouraging patterns of mismanaging money? To begin with, let us examine the nature of habits themselves.

HABITS-BEHAVIOUR WITHOUT THINKING

A habit, as defined by Webster's Dictionary is; 'a constant, often unconscious inclination to perform some act, acquired through its frequent repetition. A habit is an established trend of the mind or character.'

Almost everything we do begins as a constant effort. When we learn something through repetition, we delegate most of the activity to our subconscious minds. This way, our conscious minds are freed to go to something new. Our lives are composed of thousands of useful habits such as waking up at a particular time in the morning and fulfilling our job responsibilities. Even perception itself is a habit.

Unfortunately, habits do not discriminate as to what is good or bad for us. Anything we repeat can become a habit. A daily drinking spree can become automatic just because that is the way we have always done it.

FINANCIAL HABITS- A SPECIAL TYPE OF HABITS

The following is an annotated list of some common financial habits. You can add others to the list.

- Hiding your pay slip from your spouse
- Declaring your pay slip to your spouse
- Going for a drinking spree upon receiving your salary
- Borrowing for consumption or borrowing for productive purposes
- Stealing small items from your work place to sell.
- Clinging to high expenditure life style when your income has decreased
- Envy for your neighbors
- Making empty phone calls
- Gambling with the hope to win one day big cash
- Impulse buying
- Not consuming all your income monthly
- Giving out money unnecessarily and anyhow (slash funding)
- Buying things which you never use in future
- Procrastinating expenditure on your growth e.g. your education

- Stingy with your money (miser)

- Giving money to your visiting relatives when your spouse is not seen.

- Giving money to your spouse to eventually give your visiting relatives.

- Going on a drinking spree before reaching home after pay.

- Laziness, that is, feeling lazy to increase your income.

- Workaholics, that is, overworking to increase your income

- Bribing others to obtain financial advantage.

- Desire for quick bugs

- Not setting financial goals.

YOUR HABIT-CONTROL ACTION PLAN

It often takes about three weeks to break a habit. Allow yourself at least that long to uproot your behavior and replace it with a more effective pattern. I know of one famous man who was a chain smoker and later decided to change that habit. After three weeks, he started hating the aroma of cigarettes. He no longer smokes now because he committed himself fully to change this habit which took away a sizable amount of his income monthly apart from the usual health concerns.

Choose one bad money management habit you have, such as impulse buying. Decide now to change the habit. The longer you postpone changing, the more likely you are to forget about it. You may have learned to be comfortable with your discomfort; but remember; even a carpeted rut is still a rut.

1. *Write down the habit you want to change.*

Example: impulse buying

Habit: _____

2. *Write your goal in a finished form.* Focus on the results, not on the process. For example, rather than having as a goal, 'prepare my budget' have as a goal, 'my revenue and expenditure are traceable! Visualizing the end result will keep you motivated. Many times the process you must undergo is not that pleasant. Doesn't it feel better to picture yourself tracing all your expenditures rather than to picture yourself recording each and every expense? Take a few moments now and write your goal in terms of your overall objective.

Example: I save 10% of my income monthly.

Goal: _____

3. *Make your result measurable.* How will you know when you have improved your money management skills? Write down how you will measure your results.

Example: I am able to trace all my expenditure monthly.

Goal: I will have achieved my goal when _____

_____

4. *List all the problems you create with your habit.*

Example: when I do not budget, my money finishes without trace and I'm always broke!

Problem: _____

_____

Problem: _____

_____

Problem: _____

_____

Problem: _____

_____

5. List all the benefits of changing your habit

Example: without impulse buying, I am now financially stable and have cash to save.

Benefit: _____

_____

Benefit: _____

_____

Benefit: _____

_____

Benefit: _____

_____

6. *Exaggerate the results.* If you have previously been not budgeting, become a super-budgeter. If you used to steal, for three weeks be super-honesty. If non-assertion has been your style, become super- assertive. Since there is a tendency for many people to backslide (even super Christians do), if you become a super money manager, you should come out just about right.

7. *Allow no slippage.* The second you catch yourself granting a stay of execution to your old habit, stop what you are doing, take a deep breath, and begin with your new pattern. For example, if your goal is 'clear budget' and you realize you are about to buy something on impulse, stop. Refer to your budget and begin anew. It may take a few minutes, but you will save time in the long run by training yourself to keep to your budget in the first place.

8. *Enlist the support of others.* People will probably notice right away that you are doing things differently. Their reactions may surprise you. You may be a threat to

them at first becouse you are demonstrating that it is possible to be more organized. This may make them question their own methods; they could try to sabotage your efforts by interrupting you or trying to entice you away from your objectives. For example, your clubbing colleagues after being paid, may surely be uncomfortable with you at first. Be firm and consistent. Explain what you are doing and ask for their support. Show them that you value your money and they will respect it as well.

9. *Use affirmations*. Write a positive statement of your goal on a 3×5 card and put it in your desk. For example, 'I am a decisive, assertive person, or 'I budget monthly'. Stop now and write down an affirmation or two that you can use today.

Affirmation: _____

_____

Affirmation: _____

_____

10. *Reward yourself*. Rewards are far more effective than criticism. Focus on what you have accomplished toward your goal, not on where you have slipped. If you have a house to buy, reward yourself for having started saving for it. Treat yourself to a meal out or heap lavish praise on yourself. After you have bought the house allow yourself an even bigger reward for a job well done.

11. *Visually rehearse your new behavior*. See yourself beginning to budget monthly, saving on a monthly basis, dealing competently with problems as they arise, not borrowing in a month and paying your tithe monthly. Stop now, sit back and take a minute or two to visualize your results.

12. *Be positive*. Don't let memories of past failures interfere with your progress today. Avoid using words such as **try**,

wish and **hope**; they imply willingness to compromise. Instead saying that you are trying a start budgeting, state, 'I budget monthly'. Avoid using absolutes such as **always** and **never**. Promising yourself that you never again will let impulse buying doesn't allow for unseen circumstances. Be firm with yourself, but reasonable as well.

HOW TO KICK SELF-DEFEATING FINANCIAL HABITS

1. Write down the financial habit you want to change.

2. Write your financial goal in finished form

3. Make your results measurable.

4. List all the problems you create with your habit.

5. To build motivation for changing, list all the benefits of breaking the financial habit.

6. Exaggerate the results; for example, if you have not being saving previously, become a super- saver for three months until you have established the new pattern.

7. Allow no slippage

8. Enlist the support of others

9. Use positive affirmations.

10. Reward yourself

11. Visually rehearse your new behavior; see yourself the way you want to be.

12. Be positive; don't let past failures interfere with your progress today.

YOUR FINANCIAL HABIT ACTION PLAN

A. Pick a troublesome money management habit that you have and follow the twelve steps for breaking a bad habit.

B. Scan the contents of this book; identify the area of money management in which you need the most help. Turn directly to that chapter and read it.

QUOTES TO CONSIDER

1. Old Farmer's Almanac-Don't worry about temptation as you as you grow older, it starts avoiding you.

2. Pablo Picasso (1881-1973)- Only out off until tomorrow what you are wiling to die having left undone.

3. African proverb-However long the moon disappears, some day it must shine again.

4. African proverb- The bell rings loudest in your own home.

5. African proverb-The river may be wide but it can be crossed.

6. Confucius-A journey of a thousand miles starts with a single step.

7. Arabic proverb-Write bad things that are done to you in sand, but write the good things that happen to you on a piece of marble.

CHAPTER 3

FINANCIAL PLANNING - HOW TO WIELD YOUR FINANCIAL PLANNING SKILLS

OBJECTIVES

When you finish this chapter, you will have;

- Known what financial planning is.

- Understood the benefits of financial planning.

- Known how to prepare personal cash budgets.

As the old adage goes, 'a person who does not plan is planning to fail.' Financial planning is the specific process of setting financial goals and developing ways to reach them. Stated another way, planning represents the individual's efforts to predict events and be prepared to deal with them.

Essentially, financial planning involves three interrelated questions as follows:

- Where are we now financially?(situation Analysis)

- Where do we want to be financially, say, in the next 5 years? (goals)

- How do we get there financially? (strategies).

BENEFITS OF FINANCIAL PLANNING

As a result of the financial planning process, you realize a number of benefits as follows:

1. *Anticipation of problems and opportunities.* Planning forces you to think ahead so that you are never caught up unawares by good or bad events requiring money. This encourages you to anticipate possible problems and to attempt to identify potential opportunities.

2. *Coordination of action.* Financial planning facilitates the achievement of your personal goals by increasing communication and reducing potential conflicts within yourself and other stakeholders in your treasury journey. The process of setting goals and sub-goals gives you focus and encourages you to pursue compatible courses of action. With planning you will identify the high pay offs and low pay offs in managing your money.

3. *Assistance in control.* Financial plans may be used as tools to help you control, say, your expenditure. A detailed expenditure plan gives you specific financial goals to pursue and the means to achieve them.

4. *Providing standards of financial performance.* A comparison of the financial plan with actual performance during the planning period can be used to provide a standard of achievement. Did you reach your financial goals outlined in your plan? If not, why not? Did certain areas perform exceptionally well? Answers to such questions help you to evaluate your own performance periodically.

FINANCIAL PLANNING - WHOSE RESPONSIBILITY IS IT?

There was a woman in Sinazongwe district in the1970s who was married to a miner. She was illiterate and did not know exactly what amount her husband was earning monthly because she couldn't distinguish between some coins and notes. She was currency-blind but very possessive. She devised a way of ensuring that her husband brought home all his salary. She prepared some sticks - like those we used in grade one when learning to count -and when the first salary was brought she aligned each note to a stick. She then found a secret place to hide these sticks which corresponded to her husband's salary. Next months when her husband brought the money, she would spread the notes on the floor; each note to each stick. If they corresponded, fine the husband was saved. If the notes were less than the number of sticks, then her husband would be bitten terribly being accused of having spent it on prostitutes. This sounds like a made up story, but, alas, it is a true one.

Different scenarios may be applicable with regards to whose responsibility is it to undertake financial planning. The following are some of the available options:

1. In many families, the responsibility is undertaken by the husband and wife (married couples who are compatible). The husband and wife will sit round table and plan how they will spend the money they received, for what purpose and why.

2. Sometimes it so happens, that one of the parties may be a bad spender, while the other is a good spender. For example, some men would bring the full salary and hand it over to the wife who has to make the financial decisions and the man is simply told what has transpired. This scenario is okay as long as the wife is an excellent money manager. If she is not, this salary will be blown off and become extinct within a day. What will follow thereafter is that bills will be piling and there will be no food at home. The wife spent the monthly income lavishly and uncontrollably. Thus, the husband should confer this responsibility to the wife if the wife is an excellent money manager than he is.

If the husband is an excellent money manager while the wife is not, then the husband should take on the responsibility. The husband should ensure that all the bills are paid and an emergency fund is put in place. The wife should only be given what she is free to spend without plunging the family into financial stress. This scenario applies to a family where the husband is the bread winner, the only one earning money from selling labor. But, since nowadays, both may be salaried employees, they must put their money together and let the best money manager take charge. If you know that you are a poor money manager, let the able manager take the responsibility for the benefit of both of you.

3. For singles, they are the only ones that can make financial decisions regardless of whether they   are good or bad money managers. However, they can seek the advice of friends, family members, financial advisors and the like.

FINANCIAL GOALS-WHERE DO WE WANT TO BE FINANCIALLY

Financial goal is concerned with where you want to be financially, say, in the next five years or so. Among the common financial goals, the following can be noted:

1. Having adequate emergency fund. One financial goal that should not be overlooked is an adequate emergency fund to tide one over a period of unexpected expenses caused by some unfortunate incident such as a wrecked car, funeral, a house fire, or a medical problem. The fund may also be needed in case an individual suffers an unexpected reduction or interruption of income.

2. Accumulating funds for sending children to school.

3. Establishing a retirement fund.

4. Putting aside sufficient funds to take an extensive and expensive vacation.

5. Accumulating funds for the down payment on a home or outright purchase of a sports car.

   It doesn't take a lot of thought to add more individualized items to this list of goals. Perhaps a wedding party, cows, farm, swimming pool might even sneak their way onto some lists, for example.

ELEPHANT HUNTING-SET GOALS AND BAG THE BIG GAME

It is hard to aim the rifle if you cannot see the target. Once you know where you are going, you can focus your energy and concentration on your goal and get there faster and easier. The principle is applicable even to marriage; what exactly do you want from that marriage? Is it money, then expose yourself to people with money like presidents, Members of Parliament, Directors, Chief Executive

Officers and so on. If you want to marry a white-man, go where they are and try your lack. But if you simply sit in the village hoping that one day a white-man will come and propose marriage, it may be a far-fetched dream; an utopia.

An important key to being successful with money management is to make elephant hunting your highest priority. This means to go after your big, high pay off goals everyday and to minimize money you spend stomping on ants, those trivial details that take up much money. If you are constantly wondering every time you spend money, 'Is it OK? Is it not OK?' there can be a lot of guilt, shame, and negative consequences. A spending plan helps you connect the consequences with the choices you are making.

There will always be ants and elephants in our lives. Unfortunately, many of us who are elephant hunters at heart end up stomping ants. The danger lies in making a career of ant stomping, we tend to go after ants instead of elephants because we get a quicker kill and a higher body count. But remember, killing ants doesn't put much meat on the table. Hunting elephants will.

GOING ON AN ELEPHANT HUNTING SAFARI!

Chances are that you routinely set priorities, but do you set the right priorities on the right activities by keeping your long term objectives clearly in mind? The key to setting priorities, the order in which you must accomplish things, is to ask yourself, 'what is my payoff for doing this activity or spending on this item? How does it fit in with my long term objectives?

If you are a tenant, rental payments should be prioritized because without paying this, your landlord will flash you out and it will be difficult for you to earn money when you are not housed. Similarly, some expenses may be delayed, for example, buying a television when the old one is in perfect working condition and you want to get rid of it simply because you had it for the past five years! Other expenditures can be foregone during that spending period until the right time. What do I mean by the right time? The right time is when your income will itself say, yes, now you can buy this.

Earlier when we were staying in one room in Kamwala shortly after I graduated from the University some few years ago, my wife spotted a two roomed house on rent nearby and asked me if we could shift. I categorically said no and she complained bitterly. The new tenants occupied the two rooms in no time. After two months, they left and the house was vacant again. By then our financial position had slightly improved and I said we can now shift to your preferred house. It is the same thing when you see an advertisement in the newspaper for a reasonably priced house, car, plot or anything, but it is still above your income, don't despair. What is yours will always be yours at the right time. For example, in the weekly promotions at, say, Game Stores, you may spot something which you have liked so much going at k 1000 000 but at the moment you don't have the K1 000 000; forget it. You may be surprised that after two months the same item is even costing less probably K 800,000 and you have K1,500,000 at your disposal. Time is then right.

On the following grid, payoff refers to *value*, priorities refers to *urgency*. The uppermost left square is 1A; the lowermost right square is 3C, and so on. Low payoff, low priority items, those on which you should not spend your money on as long as you have something else to buy, go in square 3C. Items on which you should always spend money, no matter what, go into square 1A. Not only are they important, but they are urgent as well. With this in mind, where would you plot the following items of expenditure?

- Servicing a loan
- Paying rentals
- Going on a vocation
- Paying dowry
- Buying food
- Transport expenses
- Buying clothes
- Buying a car
- Entertainment expenses
- Buying a plot or building a house
- Saving.

PRIORITY

		A (DO NOW)	B (DO SOON)	C (CAN WAIT)
P A Y O F F	1 High			
	2 Medium Value			
	3 Low			

Note that the above principles can be applied to any activity such as your income sources analysis. Focus spending your money on your 1A, 1B and 1Cs. If you must buy trivia, spend less money.

HOW TO DEAL WITH HIGH-PAYOFF EXPENDITURES

1. *Build your expenditures around high payoff activities*; schedule the less important items for the money left over.

2. *Stay focused.* Put distractions aside and keep the end result in mind.

3. *Set deadlines.* Make them specific.

4. *Divide projects into smaller units*.

5. *Get help.* Sometimes you can't do it alone

6. *Reward yourself.* Keep yourself motivated.

7. *Make commitment.* Full speed ahead!

HOW TO DEAL WITH LOW PAYOFFS EXPENDITURES

1. *Delay them.* Postpone them until the right time.

2. *Ignore them.* Some expenditure is better left undone.

HOW TO PREPARE A PERSONAL CASH BUDGET

Setting up a budget will require some work, but the benefits more than offset the time invested. Mohammad Ali, the legend, once said 'before I dance in the ring, I spend considerable time jogging'. This is the same thing for those who are preparing to take professional examinations- hard work is called for if one is to pass the examinations. There are no short-cuts. How you study is purely your own choice the bottom-line being that you pass at the end of the day. This scenario is the same for someone who is interested in improving money management skills. How you create your budget is up to you. You may choose any tools available to you; those with computers can choose a piece of financial planning software, such as Microsoft Money or Quicken, or you may choose the paper and pencil route. The above worksheet is simple yet inclusive that you use to get started.

A budget is the result of financial planning. Stated simply, a budget is a formal plan expressed in kwacha. The process of financial planning is called budgeting. My main thrust here is to do with personal cash budget which is defined as a detailed budget of cash flows and outflows incorporating both revenue capital items.

The first element of any budget is your income, or how much money you receive, say, each month. This could include salary, legal settlements, alimony, royalties, fees, and dividends from investments that you do not re-invest. Once you know what your monthly income is, you can use a budget to make sure you don't spend more than you make, thus helping you to reduce the debt and freeing up cash for savings.

Next, you need to know how you spend your money. Start by tracking your spending for a month. Gather bills and receipts, and don't forget those where sellers do not issue you a receipt, though there is nothing wrong for you to demand for a receipt from them. Don't assume any expense is too small to record. It is these very small expenditures which give the biggest trouble. You will agree with me that big expenses like buying a house is well though-out before action.

Write down the expenses and break them into categories. For example, the expenses may be categorized into *fixed committed expenses* like mortgage, loan insurance payments ,rentals, Savings and children's education that stay the same from month to month. Notice that children's education and savings appear as fixed committed expenses. This is to encourage you to pay yourself first, a key to saving. Other committed expenses – the things you can't live without, like food, utilities, and clothing. Finally, you have *discretionary expenses* – things you like but don't necessarily want.

The cash budget can show four financial positions namely, short term deficit, short term surplus, and long term deficit and long term surplus. A deficit exists when your cash receipts are less than your cash payments during the period in question. Similarly, a cash surplus exists when your cash receipts are greater than your cash payments.

The cash budget will assist you to forecast your cash position so that the required remedial action can be arranged in advance. Generally, if a deficit is anticipated, some payments can be delayed or purchase of certain items deferred, that is, if your expenses are greater than your income, you will need to find ways to economize. Look at discretionary expenses first. This is typically the easiest place to reduce spending. Begin by cancelling magazine subscriptions to titles you don't read. Eat fewer meals out, or chose less expensive restaurants. Grow your own vegetables from your backyard to save money. Once you have reduced your discretionary spending, look at those other committed expenses. Can you reduce the junk refined bill with more economical meal? How about taking public transportation instead of cabs? (More details in chapter 5 of this book). For a surplus, you have got to know how best to invest cash. If you are already participating in some form of investment(which I presume you are), think about either increasing your investments now or increase the portfolio to diversify away some investment risks (see chapter 8).

The following is an illustrative personal cash budget for Mr. X for the months of January, February and March 2011.

PERSONAL CASH BUDGET

	January K	February K	March K
CASH RECEIPTS			
Salary	1 000 000	1 000 000	1 000 000
Sale of car	-	-	10 000 000
Rental income	500 000	500 000	500 000
Interest received	20 000	10 000	5 000
Any other cash receipt	50 000	40 000	100 000
Total cash receipts:	1 750 000	1550 000	11 605 000
CASH PAYMENTS:			
Food	500 000	500 000	500 000
Rental expenses	800 000	800 000	800 000
School fees	500 000	-	-
Loan servicing	200 000	200 000	200 000
Airtime	200 000	100 000	200 000
Any other cash payments	100 000	50 000	300 000
Total cash payments	2 300 000	1 650 000	2 000 000
Receipts less payments	(550 000)	(100 000)	9 605 000
Opening cash balance	(750 000)	(1 300 000)	(1 400 000)
Closing cash balance	(1 300 000)	(1 400 000)	8 205 000

Notes:

1. The closing balance in January becomes the opening balance in February and so on

2. For Mr. X, his account at the bank was overdrawn in January.

3. For Mr. X, there are a good number of sources of cash receipts. However, for others, salary may be the only one.

4. Some cash receipts such as sale of a car as well as some cash payments such as school fees may only be received or paid once as the case might be. But other receipts and payments may be fixed month to month.

5. For Mr. X, there will be short term deficits in January and February but a comfortable surplus in March arising out of car sale.

6. A total column for each month can be included.

7. Remember that your budget is a living document. As your circumstances change, so will your goals and needs even your income. Review your budget every few months to make sure it reflects your goals and see if you are saving as much as you possibly can. It is utterly essential to set a saving goal, for both short-term and long-term needs. Studies have revealed that families with savings goals tend to save more (see chapter 6 of this book).

HOW TO PREPARE A SHOPPING LIST

From a personal cash budget you can prepare a 'shopping list'. This is a list of what you want to spend your money on when you go out shopping. Interestingly, very few people have a habit of preparing shopping lists hence they end up buying goods on impulse. I am happy with retail shop owners whether in town or rural areas. When it is time to order goods from wholesalers they make sure that they have a list based on possible demand hence profit. Without this list, they will order something that they will fail to sell eventually. A shopping list allows you to control your expenditure and to be focused on what is really important for you. There will be no surprises. You even know where to go to buy the listed items.

A typical shopping list for a housewife may look like this:

Items to be bought	amount (K)
• 5 liters cooking oil	50 000
• 10 packets boom detergent paste	20 000
• 10 Bu-tone soap	15 000
• Perfume	50 000
• Hair-do	100 000
• 25kg mealie-meal	50 000
• 10kg sugar	50 000
• 2kg salt	5 000
• Fresh fish	100 000
• 5kg mixed cut beef	100 000
• School shoes for Jane	50 000
• 10 exercise books	50 000
• 5 chickens	100 000
• Miscellaneous	100 000
Total	840 000

Thus, a shopping list should be extracted from the cash budget specifying items you have to buy and the estimated expenditure on each item of expenditure. With this you will know exactly how much money to carry with you and where to do your shopping. The following points should be borne in mind:

1. Take care that the allocation for miscellaneous does not lead you to impulse buying. It should mainly be for covering up some items whose actual costs may be higher than the budgeted costs. For example, you may find that 5 liters cooking oil is going at K60 000 meanwhile you had budgeted for K50 000. You can get a K10 000 from miscellaneous expenditure item to cover the short fall without significantly altering your shopping list.

2. Prepare your shopping list in line with your income and cash budgeting allocation. Do not shoot for stars because you will never win! Stay within your income permutation. For example, some expenditure items can be delayed or foregone as the case might be.

PREPARING YOUR PERSONAL SHOPPING LIST

Using the following space, prepare your forecast shopping list for the next month. You may add items to the given list until you exhaust your forecast shopping list.

	Item to be bought	Amount (k)
1.	………………………..	……………………….
2.	………………………..	……………………….
3.	………………………..	……………………….
4.	………………………..	……………………….
5.	………………………..	……………………….
6.	………………………..	……………………….
7.	………………………..	……………………….
8.	………………………..	……………………….

9. ....

10. ....

Total   _____

HOW TO PREPARE A SUCCESSFUL SHOPPING LIST

1. Get in the habit of writing a shopping list whenever you want to go out shopping.

2. Be realistic and aware of the limitation of your disposable income

3. Don't over stretch.

4. Allow an expenditure cushion in the form of miscellaneous.

5. Review your list after shopping to improve your estimates.

6. Hunt an elephant, or part of an elephant each time you prepare a shopping list.

YOUR FINANCIAL PLANNING ACTION PLAN

A. Identify the high pay off elephants in your budget. List the actions needed to achieve these goals.

B. List the low payoff elephants in your budget. List the action steps to accomplish these goals.

C. Fill in the high payoff/low payoff expenditures on your priority/ pay off grid.

D. Prepare your cash budget for the next month.

E. Write down a shopping list for the upcoming month.

QUOTES TO CONSISDER

1. Mark Twain- Plan for the future because that's where you are going to spend the rest of your life.

2. Epictetus- First say to yourself what you would be; and then what you have to do.

3. Anon-You cannot win a battle without a working strategy.

CHAPTER 4

INCOME-HOW DO YOU MAKE YOUR MONEY

OBJECTIVES

When you have finished this chapter, you will have;

- Understood how you make your money legally and morally.

- Insights on the options available to make money

- Insights on why income fluctuates

- Been challenged as far as earning money is concerned.

Any one aged above 18 years must earn or make money except the very few who are excessively disabled to be able to do something which represents 0.0005% in Zambia. I take offence to hear some able-bodied youths who stay at home without making money on pretext that there is no employment. Some even start drinking beer as early as 06:00 hours in the morning. Some youths have excellent qualifications in their careers but are lazing around waiting for the government to create employment for them. When you ask such youths why they cannot start their own small businesses, their common answer is that they don't have seed capital. I beg to differ with this popular notion that to start business you need seed capital. It is my considered view that what is actually needed is knowledge in your area of business. Period! That is the reason why if one borrows heavily to start up a business, they end up stressing themselves the more. In the same vain, one out of seven of the inherited businesses fail within five years of the initiator's death, why?

I founded Premier College of Banking and Finance limited literally without seed capital. All I had was expert knowledge in training bankers. I did not receive any ngwee from my former employer in the form of terminal benefits and I had not build a cash reserve of any form. I started with two certificate in banking students. To date Premier College is the market leader in training bankers in Zambia. I did not say I had no seed capital; my seed capital was in my head. My friendly advice is 'Don't start businesses with capital but the business concept without capital and then look for that capital'. Start from where you are. God cannot bless in a vacuum, He blesses what you have. Do not start from the top, but start small and grow overtime. Only grave diggers start from the top. So use your talents as you are not talentless!

INCOME EARNING OPPORTUNITIES

I have studied the lives of a great men and famous women and I found that the men and women who got to the top were those who did their jobs they had in hand with everything they had of energy, enthusiasm and hardworking. Truly, most people have seeds of greatness within them, but for whatever reason they are never inspired, encouraged or committed to doing anything with what they have. Yet opportunity lies around them in many strange and interesting forms. The problem with some youths is pride. 'Me am a Grade 12 school leaver I can't do this or that'. Everything starts somewhere and every company in the world regardless of its size, started first in the mind of one person who shared it with others who caught the dream.

It is my oft-quoted conviction that we are all operating under capacity. You must start somewhere, so start where you are.

EARNING ENOUGH INCOME

Generally, there are two broad sources of earning income. You may either make your money from selling your labor to an employer for a salary or you may make your money from doing business. Few people will also make money from handouts such as government cash transfer program under the Ministry of Community Development and Social Welfare. Whichever, the source of income, it may either be described as enough or not enough.

If you derive your income from selling your labor (you are a salaried employee), your salary will be dependant largely upon your educational attainments, skills, work experience, position you hold and type of your employer. For example, a Cleaner may earn k200 000 monthly which translates into k6 666.67 per day while a Professor employed as a consultant may earn k 500 000 per hour minimum! Similarly, a certificate holder in banking working for a reputable financial institution will earn much more than a civil servant employed as a primary school teacher with the government. This is in spite of the fact that a certificate in banking can be completed in a record time of six months while you need three years to complete your certificate in teaching. Thus, the position you hold, type of employer, qualification, skills and experience determine how much you will earn as an employee. It is important to note that these are controllable variables at your disposal.

If you derive your income from doing business, remember it is the business techniques that you use which will influence your income. What line of business are you in? How competitive is the industry you operate in? What constraints do you face as you go about doing your business? For example, if you are a peasant farmer dependant on rain-fed agriculture, you will receive income once a year which will be influenced by weather conditions during the year. Further note that when there is a bumper harvest nationwide, as a farmer you receive less income because prices are depressed!

NOT SATISFIED WITH YOUR INCOME

Money is one of the few things where the economist's 'law of diminishing utility' which simply states that the more you have, the less you need, does not apply. It doesn't matter what the income level is, people always think they need more than they have. Usually, the more money you have, the more money you need for various reasons. For example, if you have more money, the lifestyle you adopt of flying first-class airlines, parties you throw, cars you drive and the like will indicate a need for more of it. The new car is great when you get it, but after six months you get used to it, and then the culture steps in and says, 'Are you satisfied? Buy this year's model with heated seats, a global positioning system, and an MP4 player'. People always want more money and then, when they get more, they end up wanting more again, because they adapt to the kinds of things they buy. People are stuck on a 'hedonic treadmill', constantly adapting to the improvement in their material circumstances. The adaptation and the escalation of goals are very substantial in the monetary area. Envy is another key factor fueling the drive for more. Everyone knows what type of a car and house the neighbors have and it's the invidious social comparison that undermines feelings of well-being in the financial arena. People always have this illusion that they will be happier if they make more money. They end up sacrificing family, health, and everything else to make more money when they would be better off sacrificing money to spend more time on health and family. My personal conviction is that financial comfort can be achieved by carefully managing the money you have. From the foregoing, I can safely state that enough money is psychologically very subjective. A person who takes home k500 000 monthly may consider it to be enough or not enough depending on circumstances such as lifestyle, residence, dependants, educational attainments, sources of income, and finally your cash management skills and abilities. The same applies to some one taking home k20 000 a day from selling roasted maize. Contentment is a crucial component of happiness and psychological well-being. Being content comes to those who see positive outlook of things, those who look at the past with acceptance and at the future with hope. Interestingly enough, having 'everything' does not guarantee contentment and happiness. For some folk, no matter what they have, it's never enough. Others, having so little, are nevertheless satisfied. What do you think makes the difference? You can, therefore, determine for yourself when money is enough for you. I am afraid I cannot dictate a figure! After all The Bible cautions us to be satisfied with what we have. Your prayer should be, *"God give me enough money and wisdom so that I cannot be tempted to steal and not more than enough so that my attention is not diverted from you."* Proverbs 30: 8-9 has this to say, "put falsehood and lying far from me, give me neither poverty nor riches; lest, being full, I deny you, saying,

"Who is the Lord?' Or, being in want, I steal and profane the name of my God". The Bible does not limit the amount of money one should aim to have but warns against the wrong attitude toward money and possessions- such as covetousness, and greed,. A wrong outlook might make people obsessive, compulsive, and addicted to money-making(albeit honestly earned) or to the accumulation of possessions. These themes may occupy so much time and effort that they become false gods.

GOOD WAYS OF INCREASING YOUR INCOME

If you are not satisfied with your income, what are you doing about it? Do you just sit and wait for manor from heaven some day? Or are you doing something legally and morally acceptable to increase your income? Think of ways to help earn income besides your normal job. I would like to think of my time as 720 hours a month. I sleep 8 hours a day for a total of240 hours; work formally 8 hours a day for 6 days a week giving 192 hours a month. My sleeping hours and work hours in a month add up to only 432 hours so that leaves me with 288 hours a month and what do I do with those hours? Maybe keeping a calendar with a schedule could help you think about ways to use some of those hours for making money legally. Hey, even within 192 hours of work, how productive am i? Don't I just do things which are even useless like dozing at work, talking senseless things with visitors, reading newspapers from front to back page, searching for food, browsing the internet, playing computer games and a host of other non-income earning activities? In passing I must sound a warning here that you do not have to overwork yourself. Here are a few points you may wish to consider:

1. *Be innovative and creative*. If you are a salaried employee, you can augment your income by doing business alongside your work. Do not laugh at your workmates who sell chickens, snacks and other products to fellow-workers, they are using a legal and morally acceptable means of increasing their income. If you are a business person such as a small scale farmer (I hope you agree with me that farming is business) dependent on rain-fed agriculture, you have to consider other avenues available to you to increase

your income. Income from rain-fed agriculture comes once in a year and it is very unpredictable as floods, droughts, locusts and so on can have devastating effects on your crop yield. In my village, a small scale farmer who produces 300×50kg bags of maize is given respect. This translates into K19.5million using 2009/10 government floor price of K65 000 per 50kg bag. Divide this by 12 months, to have K1.625 million per month. Subtract from this figure the cost of input, imputed labor costs per year (and the fact that some farmers sell to briefcase business persons at lower than floor price for ready cash), you may find that your profit margin is very minimal. Now consider, a briefcase business person who buys the same 300×50kg bags of maize from remote areas at K24 000 per three tins (approximately 68kg) in a month and sells them at K65 000 each. He would have spent K7.2 million plus about K 3 million for transport and empty bags and earn K19.5 million. Of the two, who has used his money and time wisely? As a farmer, boost your income by diversifying your income sources. Find alternative income generating activities such as operating a grocery shop, hammer mill, gardening, animal husbandry, running minibus or Canter transport business and so on. Once you do this, your annual income will be ten times your current income .Try it!

2. *Improve your educational attainments.* Generally, the higher you are on your educational attainments, the higher your salary (refer to salaries of a Cleaner and Professor given earlier). For example, if you are a Security Guard and you are not satisfied with your salary, what are you doing about it? Certainly you can not expect to earn your managing director's salary. Far, far from it. You have to invest in the most important assets you have- which is yourself. Improve your educational attainment. Don't just sleep even when you are free in that week; use that time to gain educational qualifications. The same goes to Taxi Drivers, don't just read newspapers from front to back cover while waiting for customers. Study. You have the opportunity to change your situation legally and morally.

Less than one per cent of all millionaires in Zambia are professional athletes or entertainers. The overwhelming majority are those who have become wealthy due to the old-fashioned way – they get an education, start at the bottom of the ladder, and slowly, over a period of time, make their way to the top. Along the way they continue to hone their skills, live within their means, and invest their money wisely. They live a lifestyle that requires they deny themselves some of the things they want now, so that they can acquire the things they really want in life. The best way to acquire wealth is the old-fashioned way – you earn it!

There are hundreds of indigenous role models who can sufficiently inspire you to aim higher. Personally, I have interacted with hundreds of people who had very poor Grade 12 results and very poor financial support to talk bout, yet they managed to pull through in their educational journey. Among these, is my late uncle Dr. Isreali Chikalanga (former Dean of the school of Education at the University of Zambia), once told me of his journey in the educational ladder when he congratulated me for making it to the University. His actual words were, 'you have excellent Grade 12 results to enter the University and choose any school of your choice. This was not the case for some of us. I started as an untrained primary school teacher (UT) after completing my form five. My results were not good enough to enable me direct entry to the University. From there I was trained as a primary school teacher, after which I enrolled to the University to do Bachelor of Arts with Education. Upon graduating I was appointed as a lecturer at a Teacher Training College. From there I secured a scholarship to do my masters in Education in England and finally Doctor of Philosophy (PhD). I then came back to lecture at the University of Zambia'. Certainly, he had a bight future that he envisaged and that helped him to succeed. You may also have had poor Grade 12 results or dropped before completing high school. That should not shutter your dreams. There I s a nicely paved route you can take. There is nothing you can do now about yesterday, but there is a great deal you can do about tomorrow. You are guaranteed a better future by doing your best to day, while developing a plan of action for the tomorrows, which lie ahead. You can certainly become who you want to be. All you need is personal conviction that yes you can.

3. *Reduce your expenditure.* When a company's fortunes are sour and bleak, it will reduce its expenditure to minimize loses. Candidates for cost reduction may include reducing it's workforce, reducing transport fleet, cancelling bonuses, teas, and other none essential expenditures. In the like manner, you can increase your income implicitly by reducing your unnecessary expenditures currently going on. You need to be flexible here because it may even involve you moving to a low cost house in a shanty compound from a low density population area with all the necessary amenities. You may have had a habit of hiring a taxi to and from work but now you have to use public transport or better still walk (if distance is not too long).You may have to withdraw your children from luxurious expensive private schools and fuse them into public schools. Even your menu at home has to be adjusted. You have to swallow your pride to remain a float.

4. *Control your fertility.* Some people produce so many children such that their income is always overrun. Don't produce children for the sake of producing children or to subdue the earth as a Biblical dictate. Have you ever wondered why the educated people have their children in best schools in Zambia and abroad? The simple reason is that their income is much higher than their production of children. This is the direct opposite for the poor where triplets or quadruplets are born .Theory has it that lazy men lazing around homes produce more and more children because all they can think of is sex. Get busy.

Once in mid 2010, I went to Naluama in Mazabuka district to attend the funeral of my late auntie. The day that followed, I was introduced to a number of seemingly under 16 years girls each with a child at her back, "aba mbamuka.......oyu muzukulu wenu" meaning this is Mrs........ and the child at her back is your grand child. The law prohibiting carnal knowledge of under 16 years old girls is alien here. Some boys make pregnant three or four girls which they cannot support let alone pay dowry.

5. *Change your employer or line of business.* Carry out due diligence before acting.

If your chosen career does not lead you to your satisfaction, change direction. For example, I have seen some colleagues who were trained as teachers at the University of Zambia but have never taught. They changed careers. Some became indispensable Journalists like my good friend and high schoolmate-MacDonald Chipenzi - at The Post before moving on to FODEP. Another is my student in banking Juliet Kapin'ga. She was trained as a nurse and she has now changed her career. She is doing her last subjects to complete her diploma in banking and become a qualified banker. There are numerous examples of changing careers to enhance their satisfaction. The only career you can not change would be that which require your inborn abilities. Fortunately, these are very few.

The above principle is applicable to business. If you sell airtime, the profit margins are very minimal unless you are able to sell a very huge quantity. For example, with cash of K190 000, you will make a profit of only K10 000. Now if this airtime cannot be finished within a week, it means you will fail to make this paltry k10 000 profit. The result is worse when if takes a month to sell it because you will have made K10 000 as profit in a month from an investment of k190 000 which translates into 5.3% i.e. 10 000 divided by 190 000 then multiplied by 100.

Now consider another person selling mineral water at k1500 per 500ml bottle. Using k190 000, he will order about 271 bottles at k700 order price. Each bottle sold earns a profit of k800. If these bottles can be sold within a week as the case is during hot season, total sales will be k406 500 for a profit of k216 800 or 114.1% i.e. 216 800 divided by 190

000 multiplied by 100. In a month you will have made k867 200 in profit. It is excellent business not so?

You need to open yourself in terms of the business ventures you select because some of them are not worth the effort, say, air-time. You will soon starve and consume your seed capital. While the above illustration is for two simple products, the same kind of analysis can be applied to all business options such as maize growing and intermediation between the farmers and millers, manufacturing and retailing, wholesaling and retailing, investing in equity and investing in transport business, being a salaried employee and running your own small business and the list goes on.

If your business option is not paying off, say, you have been selling airtime for the past 10 solid years without any improvement, try others. Remove the 'fikaisova kuntanshi' syndrome in Bemba language translated 'things will sort themselves out in future'. Your deliberate actions are called upon to change your situation. You need more than eyes to see excellent business opportunities.

BAD WAYS OF INCREASING YOUR INCOME

As I alluded to earlier on, income may be earned by selling your labor or engaging in some sort of business venture. In either case, the sources of your income should be legally and morally acceptable. You do agree with me that some sources are morally wrong though legally right and vice versa. This is because legality is a matter of constitutional provision whilst morality is based on what 'society thinks of'. For example, someone who has stolen money or killed someone may be acquitted by the courts on the basis of technical legal point, but be convicted in the mind of society. Similarly, making money by selling sex is legally right but morally wrong in some societies. Yet other sources are both legally and morally right like selling your labor to earn money.

Given below are bad ways of increasing your income:

1. *Trying to increase your income by illegal means such as corruption, black mailing, fraud, money laundering,*

drug trafficking-the list is endless. In recent years, news papers are full of stories of Zambian women engaged in drug trafficking for quick and easy money. The convicted women have openly testified their heartfelt regret for their involvement. Some have even been killed by the same drugs! Similarly, getting rich through robbery, money laundering will not make you raise your head high as a rich person. Inner guilt will always hound you even if you are not imprisoned eventually. As a young man, I used to wonder why shop workers at Bhagoo's Supermarket in Mazabuka used to be lined up for searching when they knock off. Now I know that most shop workers are shoplifters themselves. What they lack is the chance! I have seen shop workers in Kamwala shopping area tying 'chitenge' around their legs and then cover them with their trousers so that they can sell to marketeers at lunch time! In many times small items have to be replaced every now and then because of pilferage by workers.

2. *Trying to increase your income by stealing your employer's customers.* The following facts hold true:

- The other day I went to Autoworld Limited at Downtown Branch to have my car serviced. The workers I found there (I will not mention their details) told me the full charge by Autoworld Limited but quickly gave me an offer for half price if I allow them to do the work at my home. They gave me their contact cell phone numbers so I can get in touch with them. I declined the offer for I thought what if this was my business how would I take it.

- In the like manner, I was once given a prescription by a medical doctor from University Teaching Hospital (UTH) for medicine costing K300 000 in the chemists and pharmacies. A man and woman shop assistants I found at one dispensary chemist in Cairo road offered me to buy it from 'them' at K200 000. They asked me to go into my car and the man promised to bring it in no time! I told them that I was sorry as that type of buying was alien to me.

3. *Trying to increase your income by stealing from your employer or your customer.*

- One bank cashier was stealing from both his employer and the bank customers by rounding off amounts to whole numbers, the difference he took away. By the end of the year, he had made millions of kwacha through this unprofessional conduct which supervisors could not detect on time. Most banks prefer women cashiers to men cashiers because men tend to be so craft!

- One college accounts clerk had two receipt books, one for the college (the official) and the other his own (unofficial). These receipt books looked exactly the same with the same logo and other features. When students paid their fees, they were given receipts from the unofficial receipt book, and then he would decide how much to enter into the official receipt book. Most of the students appeared to be behind in payments as shown by the official receipt book and the College Principal took time to make a follow up as to why students were not up to date with payments. It was revealed that most of them did not actually owe the college as evidenced by the receipts they held. On further scrutiny, everything came to light.

- *Putting ghost workers on payroll.* This was a big problem in the Ministry of Education and other government departments. I had also seen it at Mubuyu farms where some supervisors would connive with villagers and on the payday, they share the money.

- At Mubuyu farms in Mazabuka owned by the Lublikhof family adjacent to my village, I was able to witness rampant theft by farm laborers. At first the owner was very safe as people used paraffin and candles for lighting. Shortly, one man discovered that diesel was a perfect substitute to paraffin. From then on, tractor drivers could connive with criminals and not less than 100l of diesel is stolen per day. Now no one uses paraffin for lighting in the farm and nearby villages but stolen diesel.

4. *Trying to increase your income by selling personal assets.* More often than not, it so happens that when you sell your personal asset to increase you income, you become poorer than before and you will not manage to replace it later let alone buy a new one. The logic is that if I put my sofa for sale to increase my income, the odds are that I will sell it at a lower price than normal. The buyer has an inherent strong bargaining power for such transactions. Frankly, if you ever sold a personal asset to increase your income you totally agree with me. It is different from a situation where I have to sell my old sofa with sole aim of buying a better one (of course I need to top up). My wise and friendly advice is never sale a personal asset to increase your income. However, you can sell a personal asset to meet some circumstantial expenditures such as to meet medical bills, rentals, food and so on as one Tonga proverb goes "kabwe nkojisi kalizyunyo ka nzoka" which literally interpreted means the small stone you have can be used to defend yourself from the snake. Your personal assets can be sold to meet your bills. Exceptionally, you can profit from selling your personal asset in a situation where you find an 'ignorant' buyer, enabling you to sell it at a much higher price and then use the proceeds to buy even a better one. For example, if someone is willing to buy my two bed roomed house in Kamwala at K500 million and I know of a similar house on sale in the same locality at K280 million, I can increase my income by selling my old house. However, these are rare occurrences!

5. *Trying to increase your income by stealing from the government through under declaration of your income for tax purposes.* This is a phenomenon for cash based transactions. Many shops do not give receipts to prove their turnover for tax purposes. The Zambia revenue authority (ZRA) has a huge task here.

6. *Trying to increase your income as a business person by using charms, 'juju' or 'muti' from witch doctors.* A business founded on charm is short lived because the owner lacks the real thing needed to run it professionally. Further, there are

lots of dos and don'ts which partakers violate consciously or unconsciously. The fortune evaporates in thin air over night (as an exercise, think of a business person in your locality now or in the past who was using charms and comment on his long term survival of the undertaking). You don't need charms to grow a successful business. All you need is knowledge. All of the conglomerates world over will convince you that charm is not a panacea to running a successful business. Moreover, from East Africa our albino colleagues are not free as their body parts fetch exorbitant prices for supposedly business booting purposes! Back here, some business persons kill their relatives one after another for the charm to perform wonders. What is the ultimate of such riches? Be wise.

7. *Trying to increase your income by gambling.* Gambling is for the losers. The industry thrives because a lot of money is lost than won. What, for instance, are the chances of winning the lottery? The odds are staggeringly against you. You have more chance of getting hit by lightening than you do of winning. Logic alone should warn us against putting any money and time into gambling. After all, the gambling industry can exist only when people lose more than they make. Yet people gamble, and soon what they thought of as fun later becomes a compulsion.

Why? Self-esteem needs seem to be at the core. Many find special satisfaction in fantasizing about winning. When they do not win, they become increasingly hopeful about hitting it next time. So, they gamble again and again. When all money is spent, they borrow, lie, and may steal in order to get another dose of this "nonchemical drug". Do not gamble if you want to be a winner! Beware of frauds,(2 Thessalonians 2:3).

Again the above list and expose is not exhaustive, add your own based on your life experiences and witnesses. What I have given here is simply a synopsis of bad ways of increasing your income. The list above is based on my life experiences and observations. Yours may even be spectacular and intriguing!

WHAT CAUSES INCOME TO FLUCTUATE

Your income is not permanent. Actually the revenue side of your budget is very shaky because of, amongst, others the following reasons:

- If you are a professional footballer, your income will be affected by a serious injury where you can no longer use your legs.

- If you wash cars, your income will cease when you are sick.

- If you are a Minister, Member of Parliament, President; your income will change when you are no longer in that position.

- If you are a civil servant, your income change will be slightly delayed because you will still be on the payroll for a long period of time but not in the private sector.

- If you sell goods illegally, your income will change when the long arm of the law catches up with you.

- If you are a business person, your income may change when the government changes tax laws, when your costs of production change and when the demand for your product fades away.

- If you operate in a certain location, your income will change when are forced to relocate.

- If you invested in equity, your income will change when share prices change on the stock exchange market.

- If inflation rate changes, the purchasing power of your income changes as well.

The above income changes may be advantageous or disadvantageous to you depending on their direction. If some changes are likely to be disadvantageous to you, then you need to be proactive. Forecast the best, bad and worst scenario that may occur as a result of the changes using the likelihood or probability and the monetary effects, that is, the expected monetary values. Be active and take the necessary steps before hand.

Add some more causes of income changes from your own experiences and witnesses. Finally, I can safely say that the revenue side of your budget is a flight bird; it can fly to unknown destinations within seconds .This is the more reason why you must wield the habit of saving to tide you over during the stormy periods in you finances (See chapter 6).

YOUR INCOME ACTION PLAN

A. Critically take ten minutes to scrutinize how you make your money. Are you making your money morally and legally? Are you satisfied with your income? What options are available to you to increase your income? Which ones do you have to pursue vividly right away and which ones do you have to drop immediately?

B. Based on your answers to (A) above, decide to act now by following the five steps of increasing your income dependent on your particular circumstances. Remember, if you try to increase your income by using bad ways, you will be imprisoned with hard labor and earn zero income during that period when the long arm of the law catches with you.

QUOTES TO CONSIDER

1. Anon- The whole world steps aside for the man who knows where he is going.

2. Theodore Roosevelt- Do what you can, with what you have, where you are.

3. Allan K. Chalmers- The grand essentials of life are: something to do, something to love and something to hope for.

4. Anon- You are young today than you will ever be again. Make use of it, for the sake of tomorrows.

5. Anon- The only way to become famous without effort is martyrdom.

6. Henry Van Dyke- Use what talent you possess: the woods would be very silent if no birds sang except those that sang best.

7. Irish Proverb- You have got to do you own growing, no matter how tall your grandfather was.

8. Proverbs 13:11 – Dishonest money dwindles away, but whoever gathers money little by little makes it grow.

CHAPTER 5

SPENDING MONEY – WHAT IS THE BEST WAY TO SPEND MONEY

OBJECTIVES

When you complete this chapter, you will have:

- A clear understanding for expenditure drivers.

- Known how to analyze your expenses.

- Known how to manage your expenses wisely.

In his 2011 National Budget, Address presented to the National Assembly of Zambia on 8th October 2010, the Minister of Finance and National Planning Dr. Situmbeko Musokotwane unveiled a K20.5 trillion budget. The budget highlights how much the government proposes to spend in 2011 and for what purposes and why. It further gives information on where this money will come from and measures put in place.

The same principle applies to you squarely. Your expenditure should be commensurate with your income in the first place. Then you need to be clear about where this money will go and why. In other words, you need to be able to identify and classify your expenditures into high payoff, that is those which confer the most benefits; and low payoff, that is those which confer minimal benefits. Suffice to say no expenditure should be allocated to those events which confer no benefits.

- **ENLIGHTED SPENDING OF MONEY – EXPENDITURE DRIVERS**

  Without a well planned spending program, money flies away like a flight bird. Within a short period of time, it is all gone without a trace. You may even accuse someone to have bewitched you (stealing your money in thin air). Generally, most people do not take inventory of their expenditures on whatever items they buy. For example, how much do you spend on?

- Transport per month

- Food at home and at work per month

- Talk-time per month

- Gifts and donations per month

- Medical expenses per month

- Parties, beer and cigarettes

- Self-development like education and empowerment

- Newspapers and text books

- Buying things which you already have and therefore will not be used by you or your relatives such as clothes, shoes, and so on.

  For most of us, income comes in once monthly while expenditures go on day by day for various items. Now consider the following items of expenditure with a view of how exactly they apply to you personally.

1. *Expenditure on food at home and other bills*

  - Many families are in financial stress because they overspend on food at home. Some women prepare more than enough food for the family and when visited. Piles and piles of food items are thrown into the rubbish bin daily. Even garbage collectors know that when they come to your home, they will have to collect 3 to 4 by 210 liters of garbage mainly food leftovers. It would be wise if you kept pets to feed these leftovers but if not this is total misuse of money. I have always counseled my wife who seems to have this habit and her response has always been that she could not measure accurately the right amount of food that should be prepared per meal or she is used to preparing more than enough to ensure that the people are really satisfied.

- Electricity bills have been hiked by ZESCO and careless use of power leads to increases in your expenses for the same. Some people would leave electric appliances such as television sets, radios, geysers, lights and so on, on the whole day even when they are not using them. Others would switch on both the radio and television set simultaneously and plays them at full blast. The same holds true to those friends of mine who use charcoal as a source of energy for cooking. Surely, you do not need a big brazier full of charcoal to boil water for a cup of tea or coffee. There is always a cost effective way of doing it.

- Water bills are another important expense at home which must be controlled tightly to manage the bills effectively and efficiently. Do not use a pipe to wash your car, running the tap when washing plates at the sink, using a pipe when watering your garden, letting leakages unattended to for a number of days and letting your bath run water continuously even when applying soap to your body. Conserve water and save money.

- Rental costs represent the major expenditure item at home as majority of town residents in Zambia are tenants rather than home owners due to historical or economic reasons. Due to lack of proven legal provision regulating the tenant and landlord relationship, rentals may be hiked at short notice by the landlord especially if the landlord stays nearby and is able to see you with nice expensive packages that you bring home. One landlord in Lusaka had a habit of increasing rentals whenever she learnt that her tenant's salary has been raised! Sometimes tenants simply do not rent houses appropriate to their financial situation. For example, if you rent a one bed-roomed house in Kamwala, you will pay about K800, 000 monthly on rent but a similar house in Chawama may cost about k300 000 per month.

Control should be extended to all other items you use at home such as detergents, bathing soap, lotions, cooking oil and so on. Be wise!

2. *Transport costs*. Most employers do not provide transport or transport allowance to employees. This means that you have to be considerate on this issue. For example, if you stay in Chawama and your workplace is in Chelstone, you will have to use four buses to and from your work everyday. That is, from Chawama to town and from town to Chelstone and vice versa. You need to spare about K20, 000 per day for transport only which adds up to K280, 000 in 24 working days in a month. Now if your salary is K500, 000 you need to relocate to Chelstone or nearby areas seriously. (Remember the minimum wage at the time of going to the press is K268, 000, thus, an employer paying you K500, 000 is legally justified and correct). Moreover, apart from the high direct transport costs that you have to pay, there are also indirect costs involved such as high exposure to road traffic accidents when you use four drivers a day and the risk of being fired for reporting late for work unless you start off at 5:00 AM everyday which again may affect you mentally. Personally, I have also seen church members who travel long distances just to attend a church service for a day when there are

similar denominational branches within their area of residence! Get wise and get closer to your work place; look for accommodation nearby your work place or attend the nearest church provided it is the same faith to have peace of mind.

3. *Expenditure on education and empowerment should be an important expenditure item.* You may be taking your children to very expensive private schools which stretch your budget. Think twice. As long as they can receive better education, a public school may be considered. Some of us went to public schools with poor infrastructure in rural Zambia but we are never an inch less educated than our colleagues from private schools in cities. We even managed to beat them when we met at the University of Zambia (UNZA). Sometimes, it may be that the school or college itself is very expensive for nothing. For example, Premier College of Banking and Finance is the cheapest in as far as training bankers is concerned and produces the best results in Zambia. At Premier one would spend about K1,800, 000 for three subjects at certificate level while some other private college charges the same amount of K1, 800, 000 for one subject at certificate level and fail to finish thesyllabus. In the educational sector, low price does not mean poor quality as is the notion of using goods. Critically scrutinize your educational expenses but never give up because it is the right way for you and your family. Recently, I counseled a lady who wanted to upgrade her qualification beyond high school. She said she had being longing to study but her income as a Sales Representative for one of the local banks was not enough to support her son and herself academically. Her son was at a private school where the school fees were really high. I advised her to transfer her son to a public school where fees are very low. She took the advice seriously. Now she is managing to sponsor her

son and her self academically without any problems. Her income all of a sudden became enough!

4. *Church contributions.* Church financial contributions if not properly done can throw you out of your budget balance. Churches in modern times are in the process of expanding. There are innumerable calls for building promotions. Moreover, pastors and other church leaders whatever their titles, now require owning drive Porsche cars and live in homes fitted with modern everything. Targets are given to church members irrespective of their incomes. At times, family targets are given even when there is only one source of income from the breadwinner. While non-payment of these standard monies may not lead to your imprisonment by the state prisons, you will nonetheless be imprisoned by fellow church members which may even make them sin for gossip.

    Further, there are other payments to the church in the form of title (10% of your income) and voluntary offerings for special projects. In one instance, my former landlord in Kamwala gave her sofa to her pastor. What followed next was that she had no sofa as she failed to replace them. Is your church contribution putting intense pressure on your budget? Are you surely compelled to make church contributions on the belief that the more you contribute, the more you earn or the more the respect you will command? Biblically, this is wrong. God does not work along those lines. God will not be happy to see you starve because you have paid all your income to the church. Get me clearly here, I'm not advocating for no or less contributions to church. All I'm advocating for is that you must exercise caution and rationalize your contributions. For example, which action will God be pleased with me; giving money to orphans' upkeep or giving money to a pastor who goes to buy a Porsche car? Remember, giving to pastors or church does not always mean giving to God. The Bible instructs us to give alms to the poor, are pastors poor to qualify for alms? Does the church have a duty of ensuring that pastors drive Porsche cars? Did not Jesus walk like ordinary men of his time?

5. *Family demands.* Another factor that can throw you out of budget balance is family financial contributions. By family, I mean a whole host of relatives you are connected to either by birth or by marriage. Some family members may make unprecedented and unplanned calls on your income. Today your mother has come from the village to ask for money for inputs, upkeep and stipend. Tomorrow your mother in law is in the house for the same; immediately she leaves, your niece and nephew from your sisters are in for school fees. What is the best way to deal with such situations?

• Get your family to correctly understand your disposable income and your personal priorities. In my life, I have seen family members who exaggerate their relative's income and wealth. These are mainly seen at funerals where these family members make a lot of cash demands on the pretext that their relative was rich. Recently a woman lost her husband in Kafue, and her husband's relatives from Chirundu demanded K5million to ferry the body for burial in Chirundu. This money was to be used for transport and meet the funeral expenses like food. They asserted that where their relative was working as a truck driver, he was well paid because there was no separation package. Meanwhile, the truth of the matter was that their relative had invested his 'good' income on houses construction and the education of his three children. Construction projects of the two houses were at roof level and slab level respectively at the time of his death. He had even not paid fully the school fees for his third child. He had also spent a sizeable chunk of money on medicals at home and abroad. The account had less than K1million. Clearly, there was a problem here. Family members to the husband correctly knew of his 'good' income but not his expenditure priorities. Or if they knew, they deliberately paid a deaf ear to his expenditure priorities.

- Delay some payments to family members where necessary. Do not just try to appease them but wield the truth of your financial commitments. Forget about what they will say about you and your money as long as you are right with your priorities. Be true to yourself!

- Refuse out-rightly certain cash demands for family members. I remember once, a distant brother of mine asked money to buy beer and cigarettes, meanwhile he is a man who does not want to do anything to earn money. He drinks beer day in day out. I categorically refused and told him that I would have been more willing to help him if he needed money for agricultural inputs or some other projects which could enable him earn his own money in future so that he could be independent financially.

6. *Polygamous marriages and extra-marital affairs for men.* Hey, some men would want to prove their manhood by having more than one wife and/ or engaging in extra marital affairs.
   The above scenario is clearly observed for some respectable small scale farmers in villages and some minibus drivers in towns. Some farmers could have two, three, four or more wives all brought in one place. By the way my late dad had four wives! Probably this is in line with the demographic fact that in Zambia there are more women compared to men, and a man must try to rationalize by helping those women to have a husband by marrying more than one wife. Or is it a source of cheap labor or to be specific free labor? This is free because of late I had an opportunity to see a family having produced good harvest but when it came

to receiving the money in town, the man went alone and enjoyed himself extravagantly and came back empty-handed. All the money for the year's work was gone within a day.

In towns, some minibus drivers play the same game even though they usually do not bring their wives in one location or house. The man would normally spread them one in Matero, the other in Kanyama and yet another one in John Laing. Added to these official wives are a host of girlfriends or concubines using the biblical terminology. These are unofficial and mostly that's where most of the driver's income goes to. The concubine's demands are honored instantly. This is not the case with official wives who at best have to be very patient to receive anything. For example, one minibus driver living in Lusaka rented a two roomed house in Kanyama without electricity. This same man had a concubine in the same vicinity of Kanyama Township where he rented a two bed roomed house electrified for his concubine.

With such arrangements of polygamous marriages and extra-marital affairs, more and more children are born. The rate at which children are born surpasses the rate at which parent's income is increasing. This means that these children cannot be supported adequately financially. It is also not easy to trace exactly what you have spent your money on. Stick to one sexual partner and you will enjoy the fruits of marriage. Your expenditure will be stable and predictable to enable you plan financially for the future. This is the Bible counsel-one man to marry only one wife or is it one woman to marry only one man!

7. *Airtime expenses.* There are people who spend about 40% of their income on airtime or talk time as it is popularly known. Aimless calls just for the sake of calling can also contribute to your financial stress. What value do you attach to your calls? Remember quantify

the value of any call you make in monetary terms. The simple question you need to ask yourself is, 'is this call so important to me that I must spend money? Some of the people are dons who if one wants to talk to them for whatever issue, let that person simply beep and they will call back. Any one regardless of whether it is a mistaken number or not. You see, it is frustrating where one beeps continuously and when you call that person is asking, 'who are you?' For me, as a strategy to manage my expenditure on airtime I only call back when I know the pager and not always. If someone has something to tell me, why should I be the one to pay? It doesn't always make sense. Yet others have created a 'slush airtime' which is dispensed at will. I challenge you to take stock of just how much you will spend on talk-time next month and get wise.

8. *Loan servicing.* These days there are a lot of companies that will entice you to get a loan either in form of cash or goods especially if you are a civil servant. I have seen companies courting teachers to get loans. Paying down for such loans is arranged in such a way that the lender collects the agreed down payment directly from the source (your employer). As chapter 8 covers in detail, there is good borrowing and bad borrowing. For example, if you borrow money so that you can buy or build your own house or to pay for your education, this is good borrowing which will improve your financial stature in future. However, if you borrow money to buy more beers, this is bad borrowing. Are you caught up in the cycle of indebtedness? Personally, you know what impact borrowed money has on your financial fitness. Certainly, you know the negative impacts of bad borrowing and learn from your mistakes. Achievers know that doing something poorly can cause the experience to do it well later on. When you evaluate and learn from your mistakes, you are free to grow. Thomas Edison tried more than one thousand

filaments for the light bulb before he found one that worked. When asked about his failure, he stated that he had not failed – he succeeded in discovering over one thousand filaments that didn't work. With his persistence, he lit the world. Finally, when necessary to borrow, borrow money from the right sources(see chapter 8)

9. *Beer parties.* This is a well established trend in my village where majority of men folk are farm laborers and participate in beer drinking parties everyday. They normally woke up and start walking to work about 05:30 hours. Upon knocking off, they head directly to the taverns before going home after 21:00 hours. Children only see their fathers on Sundays when they are off before heading to beer halls in the afternoon. For this reason, some children only see their fathers once a week on Sunday mornings. This pattern is the same in towns especially in the townships. These men do not head home straight after work but to beer halls to drink and meet friends.

    How much do you spend on beer every day? Do you always plan this expenditure? Are you like some that I have seen who when they come to the beer halls, the colleagues heap praises and the man goes to buy beer for everyone in the hall?

10. *Impulse buying.* This is the buying of goods which you have not planned. It involves buying whatever attracts your eye as long as you have the money. For many people, impulse buying is the root cause of financial difficulties. Do you sometimes buy things just because your friend is selling even though you will never use them? I have seen people who will do so just to appease their friends. They will not even negotiate the price, even if it is clear that the product is overpriced. This indirect form of assisting your friend is what I call blackmail (not in a legal sense). Huge amounts are spent on useless products to the buyer for the sake

of friendship. Do you have to buy friendship in this manner? I thought a real friend will love you for who you are and not necessarily what you do for him or her. Have the courage to say no .It is worth a dime many times. The impulse buying habit has to be changed using methods discussed in chapter 2 of this book.

11. *Use of ATM cards.* An Automatic Teller Machine (ATM) is a modern banking innovation due to the improvements in technology. The ATM lobbies are located outside banking halls, and also in many large retail stores, shopping malls and factories. The machines are maintained by the local branch.

Using the ATM, you can withdraw cash or deposit cash 24/7 even when banking halls are closed. Other services include ordering mini Bank statements checking the account balance and so on. For some people, the ATM is a blessing in disguise. I once heard a story of someone at a night club whose money finished at 23:00 hours and rushed to a nearby ATM facility so he can withdraw and drink more beers. Does having an ATM card make you fail to control your expenditure appetite? If yes, then you need to surrender it back to the bank immediately. This will provide restrain as you wait for banking halls to open. Get wise. An ATM card wrongly used can be a nuisance to you.

12. *Personal Cheque book.* Having a cheque book implies that one has a current account with a bank, though today even savings accounts carry cheque books. Cheques are a convenient way of paying for goods and services compared to cash. It has led to unplanned expenditures. Some people end up flushing cheque leaves unconditionally leading to financial stress. Take care!

EXPENDITURE SELF-CONTROL ASSESSMENT PLAN

Bearing in mind the above twelve expenditure drivers and others you can think of which specifically apply to you, complete the following questionnaire to assess how well you control your expenditure.

	Yes	No

1. Do you prepare expenditure budget monthly?

2. Do you know how much you spend on airtime monthly?

3. Do you know how much you spend on beer monthly?

4. Do you overshoot your budgeted expenditure at home?

5. Do you take interest to control your expenditure at home?

6. Have you ever bought anything on impulse?

7. Have you ever been interrupted financially by family members?

8. Have you ever been disturbed by your church contributions?

9. Is loan servicing an issue for you?

10. Is the use of an ATM a nuisance to you?

YOUR SPENDING ACTION PLAN

A. Forecast all your expenses in the next month.

B. List and allocate money for each expenditure item in order of priority.

C. At the end of the month, compare your budgeted expenses with the actual expenses.

D. Where variances are spotted, try to understand why. For example, if one item exceeded the budgeted expense, find the reasons why.

E. Revise your next month's budgeted expenses taking into account the likely changes anticipated.

QUOTES TO CONSIDER

1. African proverb – The strong ones hear the unseen. You need more than eyes to see the bush.

2. Peruvian proverb – Envy for a friend is like the taste of sour pumpkin.

3. Thomas Alva Edison (1847-1931) – All I ask of my body is that it carries around my head.

4. Anon – Discipline is the difference between goals and accomplishments.

CHAPTER 6

SAVINGS- HOW TO CREATE AN EMERGENCY FUND

OBJECTIVES

When you have finished this chapter, you will have to

- Appreciated the importance of creating an emergency fund.
- Been motivated to start saving.

Beginning your working or business life with good financial decisions doesn't call for complex moves. It does require discipline and long term outlook. This commitment can help you get out of debt and keep you from one income to next income cycle without headaches or should I say without pressing a financial panic button.

Your income is limited, and you don't have much money (if any) left at the end of the month. So where can you find money to save and once you find it, where should this cash go?

REASONS FOR NOT SAVING MONEY

1. *Inadequate income*. All that I make monthly is spent to meet my basic needs.

2. *Impulse buying*. I buy whatever attracts me in shops and on the streets as long as I have money.

3. *Family interruptions*. My extended family interrupts my financial program so much that am always under pressure.

4. *Lack of Financial plan.* I cannot realistically figure out my income let alone my expenses. I do not know how to budget.

5. *Too committed financially.* By the time I receive my income, it has already been committed to various financial obligations such as debt servicing which leaves no room for savings.

6. *High minimum bank balances and charges.* I do not save because the minimum balances required to open a bank account and monthly charges for account maintenance are too high and I cannot afford.

7. *Do not know the importance.* I do not save because I do not know the reasons why I should save money when even if I spend all today, I will make more cash tomorrow.

8. *Low interest rates.* I do not save because the interest rates given by banks on saving are too low and it is usually eaten up by rising prices of goods and services due to inflation.

9. *No bank in the vicinity.* I do not save because banks are located far away from my home. There is no bank nearby for me to open a savings account. Even if I saved I could not use my money to meet an emergency because the bank is some kilometers and kilometers away in town.

10. *Insecurity of cash at home.* I cannot save cash at home because my husband will always search for it and steal it (use it for beer drinking) and I am told banks steal money; you may deposit K100, 000 today and at the end of the month, they tell you that you have K10, 000 in your account even though you did not withdraw.

11. *Age restriction.* Since I am young, I still have much more years of earning money and I need not start saving now until am old enough.

12. *Capacity to earn income.* I have sure-fire ways of receiving my regular income through loyalties from my published book or patented product. I therefore do not need to save.

13. *Income allocation monthly.* I make sure that I spend all my cash to cover my month's expenses hence I need not save since am well covered fully.

14. *Too big family.* I have just too big a family to adequately feed and spare some cash for saving.

    Readers, these are some of the common reasons as to why people do not save. Some are plausible while others are much illogical which can be traced back to poor saving culture and a secluded financial sector.

RESPONSES FOR SOME RESPONSES

When looking at the above reasons given as to why people do not save, consider the following responses:

1. A person's income is never adequate or inadequate to save. It all takes your resolve to save. I have been privileged to interview some breadwinner marketeers who make as little as K2000 per day but still manage to put aside about K500 per day to meet emergencies. As long as they are able to maintain their 'capital' (note that this is not the economists definition of capital), out of any profits made they are able to consume and save accordingly.

2. Impulse buying and family interruptions can also be sorted out by having your financial goals in place, a detailed budget and effective communication to your family members so that they can know when to and not to demand money from you. Do not let your family members exaggerate and dictate your financial life.

3. Earning interest rate is not the prime reason for saving but to meet emergencies as and when they fall due without resorting to borrowing. Help me here; which option

is better, for me to save a little monthly so that I do not have to borrow in January from Blue Financial Services at exorbitant interest rates for school uniforms and fees? Certainly, small savings would be a better option.

4. I do not save because I will make more money tomorrow and I have stable income sources. This is a dangerous financial outlook. You certainly do not know what tomorrow holds for you. If you use legs to earn money, your legs may be amputated overnight following a road traffic accident; if you use your eyes, you may become blind overnight; if you are a landlord earning rental income, it may be destroyed by fire; if you operate a taxi business, it can be stolen at gunpoint overnight; if you are an employee, you may lose employment overnight without compensation or be shot by a Chinese investor without compensation!

5. Bank charges and minimum balances to maintain an account have been going down of late. In fact, some banks in Zambia do not require a minimum account balance or account maintenance charges have been scrapped. Further, there are other viable options of saving money such as 'chilimba' for women, at home, in your office or car. Just don't let yourself to be financially dry!

6. If you have a bad habit of impulse buying as long as you have cash, it is high time you changed this attitude. Prepare monthly budgets to manage your money wisely. Identify and classify your expenditures and make reference to your financial goals (chapter 3). Once you do this, you will not fail to save whatever your level of income.

7. I have too big a family hence I have nothing to spare at the end of the month. Learn to control your fertility. There are many family planning methods available today at each and every clinic affordably. Don't just produce children blindly; first pregnancy twins, second pregnancy triplets, third pregnancy another set of twins, and so on. It is better to have few children which you can look after adequately

than having many children which you send in the streets to beg money!

REASONS FOR SAVING MONEY

Once I was watching a documentary on DSTV involving insects which were busy making hey while the sun shined. It ranged from honey bees to termites to a host of other insects. One theme to all these insects was that they knew that they would not have food throughout the year due to changes in seasons. They had to store enough in anticipation of periods when there would be food shortage. Now if insects could know that not all days are Mondays, how much more people who are created in the image of GOD!

The following is a list of common responses given by people when asked why they save money:

1. I save money because I do not know what will happen to-morrow.

2. I save money because I receive a healthy salary from my employer or business venture.

3. I save because I know the importance of saving even though my income is low.

4. I save because I have committed myself to save 10% of my income monthly.

5. I save because all my colleagues have savings accounts, and my parents always saved money, no matter how tight money was.

6. I save money to enable me meet my financial goals like the saving for education of my children, saving to buy a house or sports car.

7. I save money so that I don't have to borrow when faced with an emergency expenditure whatever its nature.

You can now appraise the above common responses in terms of their correctness or wrongness and then consider where you are yourself with regards to saving to meet emergencies. Be frank with yourself as go you about this exercise.

YOUR SAVING ACTION PLAN

A. If you should ever become disabled or lose your job or business, you will need savings to fall back on until you start earning again. Try to save at least three months worth of living expenses in an easy-to-access "liquid" account, which may be provided by your local bank. Saving up emergency cash is easier if your bank has an automatic payroll savings plan. These plans automatically transfer a designated amount of your salary each pay period-before you receive it-directly into your account. It's automatic so you don't have to think about how you are going to deposit this month. Be a debtor to yourself and faithfully pay off this debt by deducting your income from the source leaving only what you can spend. This is the essence of paying yourself first which is a cornerstone to savings.

B. The best thing to have is emergency CASH! If you spend less than you make and stash the difference into a savings account, you won't need to borrow at all. Logically, if you live on 80% of your income, you will never run out of cash. It is a basic idea – for every kwacha you make, give 10% to God in tithe (to calm the 'greediness' and calm the attitudes of entitlements), you save 10% in a savings account for hard times and you live within your means on the remaining 80%. If you can't tithe 10% and save 10%, then start with something – it all adds up! Our ancestors didn't have credit cards to tide them over and anticipation meant survival. Sometimes the old fashioned attitudes are the best ones to have!

QUOTES TO CONSIDER

1. African Proverb – It is the fear of what tomorrow may bring that makes the tortoise to carry his house along with him wherever he goes.

2. Canadian proverb – Patience is a tree whose root is bitter, but its fruit is very sweet.

3. African proverb – A man who accepts advice is still a man who acts from his own free will.

4. Prophet Phillip Banda – If you cannot save 1 Rand you cannot save 10 000 Rand.

CHAPTER 7

SAVINGS- HOW TO BUILD A CASH RESERVE

OBJECTIVES

> - When you finish this chapter, you will have:
> - Understand the various investment vehicles available.
> - Been motivated to start investing.

In the previous chapter, I considered the type of saving where your main aim is to meet emergencies without regard to what interest you can earn from such savings, in other words, this is the type of saving which is 'interest inelastic' that is, does not change with changes in interest rates. In this chapter, I will consider saving which is aimed at building a cash reserve and/or growing over time. Because this saving has to grow, it is called investment and is 'interest elastic', that is, responds to changes in interest rates. Further various investment vehicles will be discovered bringing out salient points for each to give you a wider aptitude to select the best according to your age, capacity risk appetite, and financial goods and so on.

INVESTMENT GOALS

The truth is that individuals all too frequently acquire investments without really defining what it is they expect the investments to accomplish. When asked for reasons why they are investing, many individuals simply reply to make money; Granted, earning a return is the bottom line of any investment plan.

However, it should normally be viewed as a means to an end. More clearly defined goals must be set or chaos will result. The self-described go al 'to make money' frequently leads investors to commit funds in a piecemeal manner that produces a kind of 'Portfolio of the damned' – a group of assets that has no coherence and accomplishes no purpose. Setting goals involves more than simply attempting to make money.

Identifying investment goals is crucial to establishing an intelligent investment program, because an individual's goals play a major role in determining the risks that can be tolerated and hence, the kinds of investments assets that should be acquired. For example, if achieving a particular goal is deemed to be absolutely crucial, then certain restrictions may apply to investments that are to be acquired in pursuit of the goal. The same limitations may be less important or even irrelevant when the achievement of a goal is desirable but not really crucial.

The following is an illustrative list of investment goals that an individual may pursue:

1. Accumulating funds for sending children to college.

2. Establishing a retirement fund.

3. Putting aside sufficient funds to take an extensive and expensive vacation.

4. Accumulating funds for the down payment on a home or outright purchase of a sports car.

5. Having an adequate emergency fund to meet unexpected expenses, caused by some unfortunate incident such as a wrecked vehicle, a house fire, a house robbery, or a medical problem.

    The above list is not exhaustive, more and more can be added depending on the individual investing.

INVESTMENT RISK
There is no denying that individuals live in an environment that is full of risks. Risks of varying degrees of seriousness are always lurking nearby; the possibility of an accident while driving a vehicle; of suddenly contracting a serious disease

of having a home damaged by fire or violent weather; of falling in the shower; of purchasing a faulty computer from an unknown vender; of crashing when travelling by air; of being choked by the same food you have been eating since childhood and so on. The compendium of risks encountered in everyday life seems to be endless.

The word risk is derived from the Italian word RISICARE meaning 'to dare'. There is no universally acceptable definition of risk. Professor John Geiger has defined it an expression of the danger that the effective future outcome in a negative way; thus taking this definition, risk, then is the probability of suffering a loss.

In line with the above understanding, investment risk refers to an uncertain rate of return. Generally, the less certain the rate of return, the greater the risk of ownership. If risk cannot be recognized, it certainly cannot be controlled.

The dictum 'No risk no gain holds good here. It is also aptly said that 'risks do not disappear, they give the investor/individual a choice, which to retain and which to shade.

TANGIBLE VERSUS INTANGIBLE INVESTMENTS
Tangible investments include assets that can be seen and touched. Sometimes they can even be cuddled. They are also called physical assets. The desire of individuals to possess a particular asset is one of the important attributes that turns other asset into an investment. The more people who wish to possess the asset and the stronger their desire and greater their wealth, the more likely that the investments will appreciate in value. Some tangible assets produce current income at the same time that they offer the potential for increases in value. For example, a farm may be desirable for the current income it produces at the same time that it is valued, in part, because of the possibility that the portions of the land are in the path of economic developments. For example, some individuals bought residential plots in Kwamwena from Meanwood Property Development Corporation at K3 000 000 for 400m² few years ago when it was still a very an unattractive bush. But

now that the area has been opened up, the individuals are selling the same plots at K30, 000, 000. The price has gone so high within 3 years!

Other tangible assets produce no current income but are valued because investors feel that in future years the assets will be sought after by other investors. Precious metals, stamps, and art are often highly valued assets despite the fact that they produce no current cash flow for the owners. Of course, some individuals may receive a great deal for personal satisfaction from owning assets such as these.

Other investors purchase these tangible assets only because they feel that the assets can be resold at a higher price at some point in the future. In some cases the assets may also provide their owners with certain tax advantages.

Intangible assets, on the other hand, are those assets which cannot be seen or touched. They are also called financial assets or paper assets as opposed to 'real assets discussed above. Financial assets represent the claim of the holder to the physical assets of the company. For example if I buy ordinary shares in Copper-belt Energy Corporation (CEC), it means that I have a claim on the physical assets of the company. Examples of financial assets are Shares, Treasury bills, Bonds, Certificate of Deposits (CDs) and a host of other types. Generally, investors purchase these assets with a view of earning interest in future. They can provide both current and future cash-flows. Some financial assets, apart from providing a return may also appreciate in value. For example, when CEC shares were first offered to the public the price was K370 but this amount trebled within three months of issue. Thus, for individuals who had brought them they received a capital gain and a dividend in twelve months! It was a profitable investment.

INVESTMENT VEHICLES

Having broadly categorized investment assets in the previous section, here I consider the investment vehicles that an individual can consider to invest his money on.

1. *Savings Account.* All registered commercial banks in Zambia offer some kind of savings account with various names such as 'pan'gono pan'gono' savings account, chikwama savings account, cheque savings account, fixed savings account and so on. Further, other financial institutions like building societies also offer various types of savings products. Thus, an individual has a wider variety of savings products from different financial institutions. The factors you need to consider for savings account are:

- Minimum deposit you are required to make to open that account.

- Minimum balance that must be maintained.

- Maximum you can withdraw without incurring an over-the limit fee.

- Account maintenance fees and the other charges on deposits and/or withdrawals of cash.

- What interest rate is given on credit balances? Is it based on average daily balances, the balance at the beginning of the interest cycle, or another amount?

- Incentives such as no monthly charges for maintaining a certain minimum amount in your savings account, access to loans, access to automated teller machines and cheque book, intra-bank and inter-bank deposits and withdrawals and so on.

2. *Unit trusts.* To get the best rate on your liquid savings, look into putting part of this nest egg into money-market funds, particularly, unit trusts. A unit trust constitutes a mechanism whereby small savings of a large number of investors are pooled and thus gives each of them the benefit of a stake in a

much wider based portfolio than he could assemble independently.

A unit trust provides a medium whereby a small investor can acquire a stake in a wide spread of industrial shares. Most trusts will purchase existing shares for their previous owners but some investment in new issues may take place. A unit trust makes its units permanently available at a price reflecting the underlying share market value of the fund and undertakes similarly to redeem them. The difference between the bid and offer prices provides a 'turn' out of which expenses will be met and profits provided to the management company. A net cash inflow will be invested in newly purchased securities, and a net cash outflow will be met by the realization of the securities.

As a result of insufficient financial markets expertise, many small investors are entering the markets via unit trusts. The benefits are fourfold:

a) diversification, b) professional management c) liquidity and d) convenience.

Many of the principles are obviously correct. It is almost impossible to achieve a broad diversification in an asset class with a small amount like K200, 000 without a fund. Likewise, the majority of non-professional investors have little time to follow their investments, whereupon convenience assumes on important role. Another element I wish to add is frustration: managing your own portfolio of shares can be frustrating in bad times. Some investors might even see a failure in their portfolio as a personal failure in selecting the wrong investments.

Examples of unit trusts in Zambia include Laurence Paul Unit trusts and Bank ABC. Take time to know the fund provider, his previous performance and portfolio.

3. *Retirement plan.* Some long term financial opportunities are too good to put off, even if you are still building a cache for current living expenses. One of the best deals is an employer-sponsored retirement plan called the pension fund. These are fax advantaged plans. If you are not in formal employment or your employer does not have a pension fund, you can consider individual retirement's accounts offered by banks and mutual funds firms. Shop around for the best investment.

Many people are investors in industrial securities without even knowing it through the medium of their pension schemes. The trustees of a pension contribution of the members so that its value is maximized against the day when it will be required to support the actual payment of pensions.

4. *Endowment Life Assurance.* An endowment policy of life assurance gives the beneficiaries an agreed sum, often with the addition of bonuses, in the event of the death or on survival to an agreed date. Such a policy is therefore, for the policyholder, primarily a form of a long term saving. The annual premiums have to be invested by the life assurance Company in investments which will maintain or, if possible improve in value over years. Part of this money will find its way through the medium of shares in industrial companies, into industrial investment.

5. *Health Insurance.* This should be your first priority, as hospital stays can be very costly. Further more, most of the hospitals and clinics do not have the required medication hence prescriptions are very common. Prescribed medicine/drugs can be very expensive and beyond the reach of many. If you are not covered under a group plan by your employer, start obtaining quotes on individual policies by calling the major insurers in the country. Many products provides both inpatient and outpatient treatments with inpatients

extended to surgical operations. If you are a person living with HIV/AIDS seriously consider the exclusive coverage for HIV/AIDS management offered by many insurers.

6. *Life Insurance*. This is the next logical step, but may only be of concern if you have dependants. In fact, at the age of 25, you are statistically more likely to become disabled than to die prematurely. Disability insurance will replace a portion of your income if you can't work for an extended period due to illness or injury. If you can get this through your employer, call individual insurers to compare rates. Note that there are other products like education, funeral expenses, travel and so on that you need to consider.

7. *Equity Investment*. You can easily do this through a unit trust or individually. Technically, equity refers to ordinary shares of a limited company and represents permanent capital for the company. Shareholders are rewarded in form of capital gain and regular dividends. You can invest directly in company shares. Opportunities to acquire new shares arise from time to time when companies raise finance by means of a public offer of shares. These can be bought by sending off an application form accompanied by the appropriate amount of money. Application forms are often printed in the newspapers and the minimum application accepted is usually quite small bringing it well within reach of the small saver. It should be noted, however, that small holdings are uneconomic for brokers to handle.

For buying second hand shares, you have to go through the Stock Exchange. No person who is not a member of the stock exchange may enter the trading floor. This means that the market in securities is not directly available to persons wishing to buy or sell securities as would be, for example a retail market to the buyer of food. All business has to be conducted through members of the stock exchange who have gained their membership after being able to demonstrate professional competence and good character. These are called Stockbrokers To illustrate consider this scenario, John has 1000 shares in Copperbelt Energy Corporation (CEC) which he wishes to sell and Jack is seeking to acquire 1000 shares in CEC, a very simple transaction can satisfy both parties. Jack pays John for the shares and John advices CEC by means of a formal transfer document, to amend its Register of members so that Jack's name is substituted for that of John. The Stock Exchange is not essential to this process and private transactions may be easily set up. What is difficult, however is for John and Jack to identify and contact one another in first place and then to determine an appropriate price for the sale. The Stock Exchange provides away in which both of these things can be achieved. The benefits of equity investment are twofold: a) Capital gain and. b) dividend payment

- Capital gain is realized by shareholders when the share price rises on the stock market. For example if John bought 1000 shares at K370 per share he would have invested K370, 000. If after a fairly short period the share goes up to K1000 each, John can realize K1, 000, 000 from selling his 1000 shares. Quite a substantial gain of K630, 000. However, this gain is not certain. It mainly occurs when the company undertakes an initial public offer (IPO) which excludes foreigners in participating. When the offer is closed, these foreigners may wish to buy these shares leading to increase in demand hence the share price rises. Further as stockbrokers would always warn you, share prices may rise or fall.

- Dividend Payments is another form of reward that shareholders may receive for investing in equity. Dividend payments are the preserve of the Board of Directors. With a business which is rapidly expanding because there are abundant attractive investment opportunities open to it may absorb the whole of the profit and still require further equity finance, that is, in effect a negative rate of dividend. Careful research can pinpoint a good number of smaller cap companies with great dividend potential. You can gauge the sustainability of dividend payouts using the following benchmarks:

a) *Balance sheet Strength*. Obviously, a consistently strong balance sheet with minimal or negligible gearing - allied to strong cash flow generation by the underlying operations - is arguably the most important underpin for a company declaring sustainable dividends. Some experts also feel more reassured by the presence of meaningful physical assets (as opposed to intangible assets) on the balance sheet.

b) *Cash flow Conversion*. As mentioned above, cash flow is a key component for sustainable dividends. A useful exercise is working out the cash conversion ratio by dividing operating profits by operational cash flow. The closer that number is to one, the more profit a company is turning into cash. It's of paramount importance that investors should always determine why (and sometimes there are valid reasons) a company has not been able to convert its stated profits into cash.

c) *Profit Volatility*. It's unlikely a company that makes huge swings in profits is going to pay regular dividends. Smaller mining companies, which are prone to huge fluctuations in price for a single commodity and vulnerable exchange control swings, can produce wild profits oscillations. It might be a generalization, but investors are more likely to receive more consistent dividend flows from producers of chickens or liquor than companies mining for copper or uranium.

d) *Lumpy Revenue*. With regard to dividends, it can either be feast or famine for companies that produce lumpy earnings. What I mean by 'lumpy' is profits derived from large, one-off contracts that might conceivably be awarded to engineering building supplies or construction companies. Looking for regular dividend payers outside the blue clip counters may be risky.

e) *Cost Base.* Dividend seekers don't want to see big fluctuations in a company's cost base. Companies that have major input costs, such as copper for cable manufacturers could have their dividends prospects dampened by developments out of the hands of management . There are a number of companies (especially services, leisure, gaming and light manufacturing groups) that boast a very manageable-even consistent-cost base.

f) *Capital Expenditure.* That isn't as obvious as it seems. Naturally, a requirement for huge dollops of capex on a regular basis will diminish the chances of a company paying regular dividends. But companies that have undertaken large investments in increasing the capacity and efficiency in plant and equipment could reap sufficient rewards at bottom line to declare generous payouts for some years to come.

g) *Dividend Cover.* A high dividend cover (the number of times a dividend is covered by earnings) usually suggests a cautious outlook by executives. But a high dividend cover can also underlie a determination by executives to pay and (more importantly) maintain dividends through thick and thin.

h) *Franchise Strength.* Forgetting numbers and ratios for a minute, investor seeking regular dividend flows need to regularly test a company's 'franchise strength'. By franchise, I mean the strength of brands and service offerings. Here investors need to stay abreast of a host of issues, such as new competition, changing trends, technology advances, health issues and changes to the regulatory environment.

i) *Controlling Shareholders*. Certain majority or controlling shareholders have a propensity to pay out chunks of surplus capital. Other controlling shareholders prefer - for whatever reason - to sit on free capital. Dividends are without doubt the most tax-efficient way of transferring wealth to shareholders - whether family or management alliance who have invested significant portions of time and money into a business.

j) *Debt Declarations*. Be very wary of companies especially small cap counters that delve into debt to fund a promised dividend. Unless there is a pending structural change (i.e. proceeds from the scale of an asset) that justifies a debt – driven dividend, the ply of stretching the balance sheet to accommodate a payout is a dangerous strategy. There's sometimes a tendency – by optimistic investors – to argue that a debt-driven dividend may signal directors' confidence in the upcoming trading period. The point is that directors are still chancing their arms especially in these uncertain times.

Finally, note that equity investment is usually a long term investment. In most cases, you don't expect to recoup your expenditure within a year. It calls for steadiness regardless of what is happening on the stock exchange. For example, in Zambia All Share Index was very low during the global crunch of 2008 and also following the death of then President Levy Patrick Mwanawasa. In terms of picking directly and creating a balanced profitable portfolio, this is not so easy. The main limitation is represented by investor's tendency to sell low and buy high. This occurs because, under fear, we tend to sell, and under enthusiasm of previously high returns, we buy too high!

8. *Land*. 'Buy land. They aren't making any more of the stuff' (Will Rogers) holds well in today's world. Land is getting scarcer and scarcer by the day. All those areas that were bushes a few years ago in Lusaka are now modern residential and/or commercial areas. Most

lenders prefer to have land as collateral because it does not go anywhere, has a fairly stable value and they can perfect their lien (a mortgage). Further, land normally does appreciate in value overtime and its value can be enhanced by deliberate actions such as putting a borehole, building a nice farm house, planting nice trees, enclosing it in some form of enclosure, repairing the road to the farm, and such other similar manoeuvres which present a very interesting investment opportunity.

When buying land, ensure that the following steps are in place to avoid the incidence of being duped.

•*Check the title deeds.* Don't buy land which is not titled for it has negligible value.   Is it surveyed or not? Is it for 14 years or 99 years? Is the owner up-to-date with annual payments to Ministry of Lands, and the Local Council? Are there some arrears and how does the owner hope to clear them?

• *Next, ask for property transfer documents.* This normally includes a tax clearance certificate from the Zambia Revenue Authority (ZRA), and the new title deed from the Ministry of Lands.

• *Do not pay the full amount for the property until the procedural issues are settled.* In fact, the Zambian law allows a 10% consideration followed by regular installments. However, this is subject to agreement between the buyer and the vendor.

• *Ask your lawyer or local court to draw a conveyance.* This indicates that you have received the land you have bought from the vendor in its current state and the vendor will no longer have any interest whatsoever in the said land. Lawyers normally charge 10% of the purchase price for the conveyance but if you are not sure of procedural issues, you can let your lawyer all of them on your behalf at an additional fee. I must hasten to state that it is worth it if you are not conversant with the process involved.

Without following strictly the above, you will end up losing your hard earned cash because the vendor may trick you. Worse still if you borrowed this money to buy the land as you will still be required to pay back. I have seen unsuspecting land buyers where the vendor has sold the same piece of land to three or more people and then disappears. Be forewarned.

9. *House*. The most important investment an individual urban dweller can think of is buying own flat/house. One lesson learned in this turmoil is that if you employ a little or no leverage in your purchase, you will not be impacted negatively by the financial crisis. For example, if you don't own a house and you are dismissed from your employment, Lusaka will have chased you because most landlords require about three months advance rental payment which may be quite tricky for you especially if you are coming from an employer-sponsored house! If you do not yet own a house, you should save towards this end. Apart from providing a guaranteed stay in a city, owning a house, if you have more than one is a sure-fire source of income with minimal or no maintenance and tax-charges. In Lusaka, and other towns, people from rural areas and the small towns are constantly trooping in creating a respectable demand for houses for rent. Zambia is still a rental market where less than 5% of the Zambian populace live in their own houses in urban areas (However, in rural areas every one above the age of 18 has some kind of house though the value is negligible because they are non-tradable). You have noticed that even the unlicensed 'real estate agents' are cashing in exorbitantly in the form of 'viewing' and 'founder' fees due to shortage of accommodation. If your employer has a provision

for housing loans, please, do not hesitate and jump on the band wagon. If not, save seriously towards this end. It is also the only sure property that you leave to your children. For example, most of the landlords in Kamwala residential area are sons and daughters of their late parents who bought those two bed roomed houses at K10,000 each when then President Chiluba sold them to sitting tenants. These landlords are able to earn respectable income from rentals which is not taxed and there are no maintenance fees whatsoever. Additionally, these same houses currently have a market value of above K250, 000, 000!

10. *Commodities market.* Commodities market normally deals in physical goods like gold, copper, wheat, maize and so on. However, my main concentration is on investment in buying and selling agricultural products. We all need not be farmers plowing the fields. Some people can plough while others can work as intermediaries between the producers (farmers) and manufacturers (millers). For non-farmers, there is a possibility of achieving decent gains in the commodities market at a minimal risk. For example, one may invest K100, 000, 000 to buy maize at K24 000 per three gallons and sell to the government (Food Reserve Agency) at K65, 000 per 50kg bag. Farmers are more willing to sell to the so called 'briefcase businessmen' because these men have ready cash whilst the government takes months and months to pay. Similarly, instead of using cash, a creative business person can use barter system – take those items from urban areas demanded by the farmers and exchange for maize.

Finally, take note that these are simply a synopsis of the available investment opportunities you may consider. Please, add to the above list of investment your own list.

YOUR INVESTMENT ACTION PLAN

- If you have a few thousand kwachas to invest, consider starting with a diversified unit trust. Avoid individual shares as they increase both your risk and your potential for reward - not a prescription for the beginner.

- Give your investment some time. Don't invest in equities with the intention to pull the money in weeks, months or even less than five years.

- When you are more comfortable with the ups and downs of your investments, then you can consider increasing your investments and broadening their diversification, again consist with your risk tolerance.

- The worst luck a beginner can have is making a lot of money right away. After that happens, many decide that investments are guarantees, and they invest all they have.

- So my advice to you is to invest a little that you can afford to lose. Watch the ups and downs of the investment and become comfortable either the volatility while at the same time increase your knowledge in available investment choices and risks.

- Over time, you should have a diversified portfolio of investments consistent with your goals, objectives, risk tolerance and tax situation.

QUOTES TO CONSIDER

1. Will Rogers – Buy land. They aren't making any more of the stuff.

2. George Bernard Shaw – To be clever enough to get a great deal of money, one must be stupid enough to want it.

3. Jonathan Kozol – Pick battles big enough to matter, small enough to win.

4. African proverb – It is not only the fox, even the snail arrives at its destination.

CHAPTER 8

BORROWING MONEY-WHEN IS IT NECESSARY TO BORROW

OBJECTIVES

When you have finished this chapter, you will be able to:

- Distinguish between good and bad borrowing
- Understand the salient points on sources of borrowing
- Know how to break the cycle of indebtedness

Have you ever borrowed money? If yes how much was it and for what purpose? Who was the lender? How did you pay back; as per terms and conditions or you struggled very much?

EVALUATING YOUR BORROWING APPETITE

- Have you ever borrowed money?
- Have you ever failed to pay the borrowed money on schedule?
- Do you interact with unlicensed money lender?
- Do you feel comfortable when someone lends you money?
- Do you feel comfortable to give excuses to your lender
- Do you borrow for consumption purposes?
- Do you hate those who refuse to lend you money when you know that they have money?

YOUR SCORE

If you answered 'Yes' to any of the above, you may be a victim of self-inflicted borrowing appetite. Compulsive borrowing appetite can be harmful to yourself just like a poisonous chemical. It can cause tension between you and others. In fact, one man said to a friend who wanted to borrow money to buy a television; 'I don't want to lend you money so that we remain friends. If I lend you and you fail to pay back you will start running away from me. When I chance you and take you to the police station our friendship will cease.' This friendly advice is very fine, I have seen people who dodge their lenders and when they eventually meet, the lender confiscates the shoes, shirts and soon which the borrower is putting on. Is it really worth the price? Or is it time to break these self-defeating patterns.

GOOD VERSUS BAD BORROWING

Borrowing money dates back from the time in memorial. "Three thousand pieces of gold did you say?" said Shylock, the moneylender. The story of Shylock the moneylender is very familiar to all those who did Grade 5 English Syllabus in the 1980s. For me this story sticks to mind because our teacher of English Language then, a Mr. Mubita Wamundila forced us to read and memorize specific passages which we presented to the class.

There is bad and good borrowing. Diligent borrowing adds value to your life while the opposite takes away the value and even dignity. Economists always advise governments not to borrow for consumption purposes but for productive ones. This applies squarely to individuals, don't borrow so that you can drink more beers or smoke more cigarettes. If you borrow for these purposes, you will soon start running away from your lenders as you will not always manage to pay back. Be sure that the additional cash is needed right away and necessary. For individuals, this could be to finance emergence medical expenses for your spouse or relative, to buy food at home, to pay school fees and so on. Generally, if you have no mealie meal at home and you are a poor money manager, it is more prudent for you to ask for mealie meal instead of cash which you will squander. Don't borrow money so that you can be envied by others, the so called 'kulibonesha' like buying a very expensive car when you don't own a house or when your parents are forever poverty stricken and have no hope of crossing the poverty datum line. Borrow money to buy self-liquidating assets. For example, if you pay K1, 000, 000 per month for renting a two bed roomed flat and a house is up for sale at K100, 000, 000, you can safely borrow K100, 000, 000 from your bank in the form of a 10 year mortgage at K1, 000, 000 monthly installments. You will have just shifted your K1, 000, 000 from paying rentals to servicing your loan while staying in your own home. If you want to buy goods for sale and you have already found a buyer for the goods and you have reasonable profit after subtracting all the costs, you can safely borrow. All you need to provide the lender is the signed contract for the supply of goods to a reputable buyer and quotations from a reputable supplier. Check a scenario where you borrow money to build a house in a location which is not yet serviced hence none habitable. You cannot put it on rent and you cannot also stay there, yet you have to start paying your loan before earning any income from it. Are you going to manage the repayments? If you borrow to buy a mini bus or grinding meal or farming inputs, what risks are there and how can they be mitigated? Are they self-liquidating assets? If yes, then consider the right source of borrowing. Finally, before borrowing money, make sure to:

- Specify the purpose vividly and be prepared to answer any questions.

- State your source of repayments which must be established and predictable.

- Have ready collateral available to back up the loan.

- Show a clean and problem free loan payments record.

- Approach the right supplier of loans.

SOURCE OF BORROWING MONEY

There are many diverse sources of borrowing money that an individual can consider. The following list is given to stimulate your thinking:

1. *Family and friends* – This is the simplest of all sources as there is usually no documentation and no interest charge. It can be arranged very quickly and repayment terms very flexible because it is informal in character. There is no collateral required only the verbal promise. Normally lenders will evaluate your request on basis of your ability to repay or on the basis of your need and give you the money. For example, I have lent money to people who I knew for sure will not pay back but on the basis of the need like emergency medical expenses. However, don't be like those who pretend to borrow when in actual sense they are asking for assistance, simply ask for assistance rather than pretending to borrow when you know you will not pay back. If the amount is not repaid their may be sanctions against you never to be allowed to borrow no matter the urgency and importance of your need (blacklisted). Further, a fight may erupt which will sour your relationship. In fact, as I said earlier on, if you don't have mealie meal at home, it is honorable to ask for mealie meal instead of money.

2. *Employers* – For those in salaried employment, employers can be a valuable source of borrowing money in the form of salary advance. There is documentation but no interest charges. It cannot usually be rescheduled and has to be repaid monthly or whatever terms that might be agreed to between the employer and the employee. The employer will not usually ask for collateral because you are the collateral yourself.

3. *Money-lenders* – There are many shylocks around (Refer to case study number 4, chapter 1). These money-lenders may be licensed or unlicensed depending on the locality where they operate from. In rural areas, they are largely unlicensed and very brutal. In towns they normally obtain a money lender's certificate to operate this business. In either case, money lenders in most cases charge 100% of the borrowed money commonly called 'kaloba'. If you borrow K1, 000, 000, you have to pay back K2, 000, 000 and it is usually for very short period time usually one

month at best. Few will demand collateral. This source can be quite inconveniencing unless money is used to produce something that will bring in more than 100% profit.

4. *Micro-finance Institutions* – Zambia has of late seen the mushrooming of micro-finance Institutions. These are highly formal, but interest rates are very high due to high perceived risk of default. They mainly concentrate their lending to salaried employees where the amount of loan is deducted directly from source. The amounts of loans granted are usually very low not exceeding K5, 000, 000. Documentation required include three months pay slips, confirmation letter from your employer and sometimes bank statements. Loan processing period is short when compared to other financial institutions.

5. *Government* – This is also another source of borrowed funds for supported profits. For example government provides loans through the Citizenship Economic Empowerment Commission (CEEC), youth projects funding through the ministry of sports and youths, agricultural support to small scale farmers through the fertilizer input support program under the Ministry of Agriculture. There is no collateral required; however accessing these funds has been a big challenge to who would-be borrowers.

6. *Commercial banks*-Borrowing from the commercial bank may take the form of a loan, overdraft or discounting bills. These are formal arrangements where the credits standing of a potential borrower is critically examined before money is released. Further, a lot of documentation is involved including longer lead times, that is, from application to approval. Commercial banks usually require the following information from individual potential borrowers.

   - Letters of application for the loan stating amount, purpose and period.

- Letter of commitment of employer to channel salary and/or benefits through the commercial bank account

- Pay-slip

- If not in employment, state source of repayments and provide proof of income.

- Security – photocopies of title deeds for the house offered as security.

- Valuation reports done by valuers on the bank's approved list.

- Personal profile age, qualification, experience, position, nationality.

- Terms of employment, that is, permanent or contract.

- Banks accountholder for at least 6 months.

- If on contract submit latest copy of the contract.

- The interest rate, say, 29% per annum.

- Maximum repayment period 3 years.

- Amount given K10, 000, 000 and above.

HOW THE MONEY WILL BE USED

You need to show the lender how you will use the money. Give amounts and totals for each category like this:

LOAN REQUEST

	K' 000
• Amount requested	30, 000
• Owners investment (stake)	45, 000

• Other investors   _____-

Total   75, 000

Use of funds:

• Purchase of maize (via cashflow)   60, 000

• Transport (via estimates)   9, 000

• Labor (via estimates)   6, 000

Total   75, 000

REPAYMENT

Term: K140, 000, 000 for 36 months. Rate: Base + Risk Premium Principal and Interest

Repayment source: - cash flow

Collateral offered:

. 3 bed roomed house   200, 000

. 10 000 ordinary shares   5, 000

. 2.5 Toyota Chaser Car   30, 000

. 21 Acres farm   45, 000

Total   280, 000

PARAMETERS FOR EVALUATING YOUR LOAN REQUEST

1. *Personal Data*

- Age – gives the economic life, and the productive years of life.

- Education qualification – Indicates the probability of higher income and ability to service and repay the loan.

- Marital status – Indicates a greater need of settlement and lesser tendency to default.

- Number of dependants – has impact on monthly outflow which translates into reduced ability to repay

- Mobility of the Individual – affects the borrower's repayment capacity and also his willingness to repay.

2. *Employment Details*

- Employment status – Income of self employed is not as stable as that of a salaried person.

- Designation – People at middle and senior management levels tend to have higher income and stability.

- Gross monthly income – affects your ability to repay.

- Number of years in current employment – indicates stable income.

3. *Financial Details:*

- Details of the borrower's assets – includes land and building as well as the worthy of the borrower's security.

- Margin or percentage of financing by the borrower – Generally the more the borrower's investment, the less the amount of the loan.

   Other details include:

- The presence and percentage of the collateral which provides additional security.

- The presence of the guarantor which provides additional security.

- Account relationship.

- Status Symbols and lifestyle.

COLLATERAL

Collateral is your assets which may be liquidated by the lender if you don't repay your loan. It is the secondary method of loan repayment, the first source is cash-flow (from salary, business, investments, and so on). Other personal assets to be considered include Ordinary shares of a Company at current market value and real estate such as a house. Lenders like real estate because it doesn't go anywhere, have a fairly stable value and they can perfect their lien (a mortgage). Lenders may recover all or a large percentage of the loan if the real estate goes to foreclosure, you should be aware that lenders discount the value of your collateral, and the discounted amount must at least equal to the loan request. Each lenders formula for discounting collateral will vary. Take, for example, a K200, 000, 000 two bed-roomed house, lender A may discount it by 30%, so it counts as K140, 000, 000, Lender B may discount it by 50%, counting it as K100, 000, 000. Be sure you understand your lender's method of discounting. Further, note that 20-50% of your money usually be invested but it depends on many factors such as collateral offered, the purpose of the loan and your repayment ability.

MODEL LOAN APPLICATION LETTER

The following is an illustration of a model application letter for a loan.

John Tembo
P.O BOX 31927
LUSAKA

27TH April 2010.
The Consumer Credit Manager
ABC Bank

P.O BOX 35182
Lusaka
Re: **LOAN REQUEST FOR K30, 000, 000**

Dear Sir,

With over 10 years of experience in the agro-business, I am requesting a loan to enable me execute the contract I signed with PCBF Ltd on 18th November 2009 to supply 200+/- tons of sunflower seed. Please, refer to the attached contract.

The sunflower seed has already been organized in Hapwaya and Mugoto areas of Mazabuka district. Am investing K55, 000, 000 and requesting a K30, 000, 000 short term loan from your bank. The breakdown of funds is attached.

I would like three months to repay the loan using cash-flows from the business. My secondary source of repayment will be from collateralized items worth K450, 000, 000 offered as collateral for the loan. As a civil servant, my other source of repayment will be from my personal earnings.

I have banked with you since 2004, account number 0482900 but have never borrowed.

If you have any questions or need more information, please contact me immediately (0977 000001).

Respectfully submitted,

John Tembo.

PERSONAL FINANCIAL STATEMENT

This is a statement showing the condition of an individual at a particular point in time just like the balance sheet of a limited company. This is illustrated below: -

Personal Financial Statement Showing the Condition of:

John Tembo

House No 15 Musi Road

New Kamwala
Lusaka.

CASH	K' 000
. Cash in hand:	3, 500
. Cash at Bank:	17, 000
MARKETABLE SECURITIES	
. Ordinary shares (ZANACO) 10 000 at K570	5 700
. Ordinary shares (CEC) 3500 at 500	1 750
. Farmland (21 Acres)	35 000
. Other Assets: Motor vehicle Toyota Chaser	30 000
Other personal effects	10 000
Total assets at market value	102, 950
Less liabilities	-
Net worth	102, 950

BREAKING THE CYCLE OF INDEBTEDNESS

For most adults, paying down debt is the first step towards freeing up cash for the financial protection, security that they need. Analyze your spending for a month to see where your income goes. If you are spending more than you make, you need to find ways to economize. You may wish to consider the following strategies:

1. Think about areas where you can cut back. These may include renting a cheap house, driving a second hand car, shifting your children from very expensive private schools to government schools. Even the type of mealie-meal you eat at home has a tremendous impact on your expenses. For example, most people would prefer breakfast mealie-meal costing about k55000 per 50kgs to 'magaiwa' direct from the hammer mill at about k2000 per 25kgs thought the latter is much better healthwise than the refined breakfast mealie-meal. For a family of four, we were using about 50kgs of breakfast mealie-meal per month for a total cost of k110 000. Recently, we went to visit the Riverview Wellness Centre in Kafue where we were exposed to literature on health foods. From then, we changed from breakfast to 'mugaiwa' and I can confess that we only spend about k12000 per month despite its rich nutritional value. Lately, I used to spend about k120 000 per week for lunch on junk foods at work. I changed my strategy and now I eat home prepared healthy nutritious foods and am able to spend less than k20 000 a week. Now I feel sorry when I see colleagues at work rushing for junk foods on Cairo Road! Do yourself a favour; add up how much you spend on meals and you will be surprised to learn that you spend more than k100 000 a week just on lunch at work. Experiment by bringing your lunch to work starting with four days in a week. This will be an astronomical boost to your savings apart from the fact that you will be more productive at work as the issue of chasing for food will be the thing of the past. You will even be eating whole foods compared to these refined junk foods which you force on your body everyday. When am out I watch friends and think, hey, how

often they buy chicken and chips. Chicken and chips at k15 000 multiplied by 24 gives k360 000 per month multiplied by 12 months gives k720 000 per year! These are things you can prepare at home if you are addicted to them at 80 per cent less the cost. Just buy three chickens for k40 000, pocket of potatoes for k30 000 and 2.5l cooking oil at k20 000. You will have chicken and chips at lunch for 24 days in a month for k90 000! Off the counter junk foods always cost more apart their being not healthy. You need to think outside the box to be an excellent money manager.

2. Restrict yourself to cash-spending system only on necessities. Once cash is gone, it's gone – no more spending. Stop contracting any more debt. It's less like mopping water when the tap is open, you will never succeed in drying up the place. You need to close the tap first and then mop. Therefore, you need to stop contracting further debt by critically examining what have been the major items that plunged you into a cycle of indebtedness. Prune some of these expenditures with the exception of these which are really necessary. Sometimes, it is more prudent to deny yourself some non-urgent things like new shoes, clothes, and so on until you get the debt completely paid off. Live in a tight budget and face frustrations for a moment but know for sure that the relief in the end is going to be tremendous. Also read articles and books on money like this one and learn the loops.

3. Consider exchanging expensive debt for a more reasonable one which you can easily plan for. For example, exchange an overdraft which is payable on demand at variable interest rate for a loan which is not.

4. Consider selling your big and expensive item to completely pay off the debt. For example, you may sell your five bed-roomed well furnished house to clear a debt and then buy a two bed-roomed one.

5. Negotiate with your lender not to add anymore interest to the principal.

6. Negotiate for debt cancellation. It has worked for Highly Indebted Poor Countries (HIPC), Zambia inclusive.

YOUR BORROWING ACTION PLAN

A. If you wish to get a loan from a Bank, ask the lender the following questions:

- What type of real estate do you accept as collateral?

- What percentage of the value are you willing to lend?

- Are there any particular characteristics which would disqualify the real estate from financing (well, septic systems, design, usage, and so on)?

- Are there any environmental concerns?

B. Construct your personal financial statements as per today.

QUOTES TO CONSIDER

1. F P Jones – Experience is that marvelous thing that enables you to recognize a mistake when you make it again.

2. John Paul Getty (1892-1976) – If you owe the bank $100, that's your problem. If you owe the bank $100 million, that's the banks problem.

3. Phillipines 4:12-13 – The secret of contentment.

CHAPTER 9

FINANCIAL DECISIONS – HOW DECISIVE ARE YOU?

OBJECTIVES

When you have finished the chapter, you will be able to:

- Evaluate how decisive you are

- Make quality financial decisions

- Improve your decisiveness

- Apply several powerful strategies to help you make your next decision.

Think about the decisions you make. Are they based mostly on reason, rational thinking, and logic, or are they based on emotions and passion? Which way of thinking seems to dominate you? Is there a right balance between these motives, and if not how can you find it?

How decisive are you? Write down a number from 1 to 10, number 1 being the least decisive and number 10 the most decisive: _____. If you are like some people, you may have felt the urge to turn to others for their opinions: 'How decisive do you think I am? Do you think I'm a 5 or 6, or maybe a 7? If you wanted to ask someone else, subtract 3 points from your score on the following questionnaire.

HOW DECISIVE ARE YOU?

	Often (1)	Sometimes (2)	Rarely (3)	Never (4)
1. Do you have second thoughts after making decisions?	____	____	____	____
2. Do the opinions of others unduly influence your decisions?	____	____	____	____
3. Do you procrastinate on making decisions?	____	____	____	____
4. Do you agonize over making difficult decisions?	____	____	____	____
5. Do you bog down considering so many details that its hard for you to decide?	____	____	____	____
6. Do you put a kwacha's worth of energy into making a one-ngwee decisions?	____	____	____	____
7. Have you missed opportunities because you waited too long to decide?	____	____	____	____
8. Do you let others decide for you on choices that are really yours to make?	____	____	____	____
9. Did you hesitate as you answered these questions?	____	____	____	____

YOUR SCORE

Give yourself 1 point for each often you ticked, 2 points for each sometimes, 3 points for each rarely, and 4 points for each never. Add up your points and find your score on the scale below.

32-36: Most likely, your life is working the way you would like it to. You have long term goals, you take responsibility for your choices in life, and you are quite decisive.

20-31: Making decisions may be uncomfortable for you. Sometimes you are hot, sometimes you are cold when it comes to making decisions. To be more consistently decisive, look for tips in the chapter. *Below 19*: You need to be more decisive, chances are you are sitting on a major decision right now. You may be hoping it will go away or that someone else will make a decision for you. To gain more self confidence in your natural decision making ability, apply the strategies in this chapter.

Every day make hundreds of decisions. The quality of your life equals the sum total of those decisions: whether or not to study, what to eat at lunch, when to go for work, whether to change jobs or ask for a raise and so on.

The results you make are the results of previous decisions you have made and past experience you have had. When you are confronted with a decision, your inner computer scans your memory banks for similar situations and bases your decision on what you have learned in the past. For example if an exam you see a question that you have revised previously, you remember what steps you used to solve it. You decide quickly what to do.

The times when you have trouble deciding are when you scan your past experiences and discover conflicting information, such as when you made the wrong choices, or when you worry about what others will think of your decisions. In these cases, it is necessary to examine your belief systems, set goals and clarify your values, make decisions appropriate to what you value in life. Do you value education, career enhancement, self-improvement, physical fitness & wealth? What decisions are you making regarding those things? Align the way you live and work with what you value.

HOW TO IMPROVE YOUR DECISIVENESS

Write down a decision you have wanting to make;

Follow each of the steps below, and by the end of this section you may be pleasantly surprised to discover that you have made your decision.

1. *Clearly define your goal.* Make your goal specific and measurable. For example, instead of saying that you want

to make more money write down that you want to make at least K1, 000, 000 in a month.

2. *Research.* When making a decision use both primary and supplementary sources of information. Primary sources provide you with valuable first hand information. For example, when you are undertaking the decision whether to be an accountant or not, you consult an accountant or two regarding the benefits of the accountancy profession and talk to other several people like career advisors. Then read supplementary sources of information for a good overall picture on the subject under consideration. For example you read accountancy books and magazines, job prospects for accountants in newspapers and magazines.

List some primary sources you can consult for the decision you want to make.

_____

_____

_____

_____

_____

_____

List some supplementary sources that would be helpful for you to read.

_____

_____

_____

_____

_____

_____

As you conduct your research, recognize the point of diminishing returns. If you attempt to consult all the experts in the field and read all the available material, the return on your invested time will begin to diminish. Sooner or later you simply have to make a decision.

3. *Evaluate the risk.* Sometimes people are afraid of making decisions because they fear the consequences of such decisions. If this is the case, ask yourself what is the worst thing that could happen if I decide to go a certain way? If the worst is very bad don't dwell on it; put some more research time into your decision and find a few more alternatives. Often the worst thing that can happen is that you will learn from the experiences and that is not a serious consequence. Mistakes can be stepping stone to wisdom.

Examine the worst that can happen if you make the wrong decision.

_____

_____

_____

_____

_____

_____

At one time, I was deliberating on whether to change my job or not. By the way I am employed by the company which I founded. While not changing my job meant low salary, I realized that the rewards of not changing my job were worth the risks. As it turned out, not changing my job was a wise decision. I have assisted many viable but vulnerable students to get an education through my scholarship program and I have been able to advance in my studies which have been my goal. Further, it has given me enough time and money to write many books of which this one is among them. If I changed my job, yes, I would have enough money but not enough time to do these things.

4. *Avoid paralysis of analysis*. If you go over and over things in your mind when you try to make a decision, if you torn this way and that by conflicting thoughts. you may be suffering from paralysis of analysis. Stop mulling over your problems. Sort out your thinking. To avoid circular thinking, write down all your reasons against it, compare the pros and cons and make your decisions,

Goal: _____

_____

Decision: _____

_____

	for	weight	against	weight
1.				
2.				
3.				

Alternatives

_____

_____

_____

_____

_____

5. *Ask the world's greatest authority*. Tune in to your own genius and natural decision making ability. Regarding the decision you want to make, ask yourself, 'what would the world's greatest authority advice me in this situation? This approach helps to detach you from a limited viewpoint and tap into that inner brilliance that knows what is best for you.
   What would the worlds greatest authority advice you about your decision?

6. *Do something*. Army officers are advised that when they are in danger, any action, no matter how poorly conceived or poorly executed is preferable to no action at all. In other words, do something.
   It might be that you decide not to decide the present. If this is the casa, give yourself a time limit for when you will make a choice. A story is told of how this strategy worked well for a husband and wife who were considering a separation. They felt that both of them were too emotional at the time to think clearly, so they postponed their decision for three months. Since the pressure was off for a while, they found it easier to communicate and began to enjoy each other more. When it came to time to decide on the separation, they chose to stay together. Whatever you do, decide something. If you are in a dark room and you do nothing, you remain in the dark. But if you feel for the wax and start to move along it, eventually you will find the doorway, a window, or a light switch.

YOUR FINANCIAL DECISION ACTION PLAN

Use the above six points strategy on the next decision you want to make.

QUOTES TO CONSIDER

1. Robert Schuller - You don't have a problem- you just have a decision to make.

2. Leib Lazarus – who has confidence in himself, will gain the confidence of others.

3. Martin Luther King, Jr. (1929-1968) – Faith is taking the first step even when you don't see the whole staircase.

4. African proverb – An elephant tusks are never too heavy for it.

CHAPTER 10

FINANCIAL FITNESS – HOW FINANCIALLY WELL ARE YOU?

OBJECTIVES

- When you finished this chapter you will have been able to:
- Define what financial fitness means to you.
- Evaluate yourself whether or not you are financially fit.
- Distinguish between financial success and failure.

To me financial fitness is to be like a well prepared gourmet meal. All essential ingredients are key to ensuring sustainability and growth. These ingredients include clearly understanding my relationship with money, correct financial habits, consistent budgeting, adequate income from legal and moral sources, enlightened expenditure, and restraint on borrowing coupled with powerful decision-making. The following are the principles that I have been using to be financially fit:

1. *Controlling Money*. I correctly understand the relationship between money and myself. I control money rather than money controlling me. For me, money is not a necessary evil but my servant. In my life, I have seen some people who are controlled by their money rather than them controlling money. For example, if when you get paid, all you can think of is to drink beer and only report for work when money is finished, then money is your master and you are its servant who has to dance to its tune.

2. *Financial habits.* I have excellent financial habits. I am very matured and experienced to distinguish between good and bad financial habits. I reinforce good ones and throw away the bad ones. For example, I don't envy, impulse buy, clubbing and I have no 'slush fund'.

3. *Financial planning.* I have always set financial goals that I have to achieve within a specific time period. I always prepare an intelligent budget clearly describing my revenue and expenditure, including the measures I have to put in place to increase my revenue to squarely meet my budgeted expenditure without resorting to borrowing or pressing a panic button.

4. *Earning money.* I earn money legally and morally. I am satisfied with my income. I meet my financial obligations without any trouble. I live within my means hence I am self -sufficient; I don't shoot for stars but set realistic goals. I have working knowledge of my income sources and certainly know what to do to increase my income.

5. *Spending money.* I undertake enlightened spending of my money. My money goes to areas which I have prioritized in terms of pay-off to me. Items with the greatest pay-off for my financial protection and security get the largest share while low items are only considered when there is a surplus of cash.

6. *Saving money.* I am a firm believer that an unfortunate incident may strike at any time without warning. I have made a personal commitment to save regularly. Specifically, I save more than 10% of my monthly income. I always have at least three months living expenses in my emergency savings account. I am able to meet emergence medical expenses, car maintenance expenses, transport expenses to funerals when a relative dies and so on without borrowing! I have made savings one of my eminent financial habits.

7. *Investing money.* I invest my surplus cash diligently. I have a working knowledge of the many investment vehicles specifically available to me and their risk-return

relationship. Where I am lagging behind, I always take time to seek professional advice. This allows me to always take calculated risks. I have always held a diversified portfolio of investments and I am uncomfortable to earn more than 100% profit because my conviction is for me to earn money slowly and joyfully while learning valuable lessons in the process for my financial stability.

8. *Borrowing money.* Though there is good and bad borrowing, I have never taken trouble to borrow money. I always live within my means as a guiding rule and plan my money well in advance taking into account any eventualities that may arise. Don't misunderstand my advice; I am not implying that all borrowing is bad. There is good borrowing as discussed in chapter 8. Despite this, the safest position is not to borrow at all.

9. *Financial decision-making.* I am very decisive and assertive financially. I am not over influenced by anyone for my financial decisions. So far I can't remember any financial decision which I made in the past for which I regret. I am a champion of my financial decisions.

HOW FINANCIALLY FIT ARE YOU?

Readers, the above nine principles are key areas of concern if you want to be financially fit. The goodness with these principles is that they are within your control. They are internal to you. The questionnaire that follows is designed to help you think about yourself in those terms. You will see that there is no "scoring system" as such. This particular questionnaire is more open-ended. Instead of seeking a numerical score, you should go through the questions, answering them as fully as possible. Then you decide for yourself what your answers mean - what they are telling to you. In this way, the questionnaire is designed to help you to explore and examine yourself, rather than to measure yourself. Incidentally, it can be very helpful to go through the questionnaire with a partner - a friend or colleague, for example. In this way you can take it in turns to ask the questions, and follow up the answers with supplements, asking for more information or examples, giving feedback on how you see other person, and so on.

1. **YOUR RELATIONSHIP WITH MONEY**

- Do you clearly understand your relationship with your money?

- What steps do you take to ensure that you are in total control of your money, rather than allowing money to control or manipulate you?

- What do you know about the way other people feel about your relationship with your money? Other people should include relatives, lenders, employers, friends, colleagues.

2. **FINANCIAL HABITS**

- Are you stingy with your money?

- What percentage of your income do you save monthly?

- Do you envy other people's lifestyles?

- Do you hide your pay-slip from your spouse?

- What do you do to ensure that you have positive financial habits?

3. **FINANCIAL PLANNING**

- Do you prepare your personal budget?

- How good are you at financial planning?

- To what extent are you consciously aware of your own financial goals?

- Who influences your financial planning?

4. **EARNINGMONEY**

How do you make your money?

- Are you satisfied with your income?

- If you are not satisfied with your income, what are you doing to increase it?

- What incidents may stop you from earning your income?

- Have you taken time to brainstorm on how you will survive if your income stopped for the next six months?

- Have you ever used an under-hand method to increase your income?

- How do you compare your income with your family?

5. **SPENDING MONEY**

- What do you spend your money on?

- How do you waste your money?

- What expenditure items take the greatest share of your income?

- Do you take interest to control your expenditure?

- Do you track your expenses?

- Do you plan your expenses?

6. **SAVING MONEY**

- Do you save money?

- How much do you save?

- What should you save for?

- Where do you save your money?

7. **BORROWING MONEY**

- Do you borrow money?

- What do you borrow money for?

- Where do you borrow money from?
- Are interest rate changes of concern to you?

8. **INVESTING MONEY**

- Do you have investment goals?
- Do you know what investment vehicles are available to you?
- Do you have any type of real estate?

9. **FINANCIAL DECISION MAKING**

- Can you think of some recent example of good and bad financial decisions you made?
- Can you think of examples of occasions on which you

   - Preferred to rely on the guidance of an expert rather trust your own judgment?

   - Preferred to trust your own judgment rather than rely on the guidance of an expert?

   - How decisive are you?

FINANCIAL SUCCESS

Financial success is a surrogate of financial fitness. The years of experience and the skills you develop while in employment should of necessity gloom you to successfully operate and manage your own undertaking unless if you are a failure in your job. Your employment should be your 'business school' where you graduate with requisite skills and abilities. Learn the loops or learn how to fish and then go out fishing yourself. In fact my research has shown that some Small Medium Enterprises die within five years upon the death of the founder mainly because the new owners sideline the core personnel who were making it tick. A total stranger is put at the helm of authority to dictate what has to be done. If there was a way I would love to see core personnel continue running and managing the business while the new owners take the shareholder position even if a business is not incorporated for the sake of continuity. The following is a list of what I call financial success for a former salaried employee.

1. If you were employed as a minibus driver, after leaving your employer you must run your own fleet of buses.

2. If you were a professional footballer, upon hanging your boots you must run your own soccer academy.

3. If you were a teacher, after leaving your employer you must run your own school.

4. If you were a lecturer, upon leaving your employer you must start running your own college like me.

5. If you were a banker, when you leave your employer you must run your own bank or microfinance institution like Mr. Friday Ndhlovu of Investrust Bank.

6. If you were a band member, when you leave the band you should form your own band like many of Koffi Olomide's former band members such as Fally Ipupa.

7. If you were a mechanic, you must run your own workshop after leaving your employer.

8. If you were a broker, you must run your own brokerage firm after leaving your employer.

9. If you were a soldier or police officer, you must run your own security firm when you leave your employer.

10. If you were a shop assistant, you are expected to operate and run your own shop when you leave your employer.

11. If you were a tenant, now become a landlord.

12. If you were a farm laborer, now own your own farm.

13. If you ere a radio personality, now own your own radio station like Matteo Johnson Phiri of The Happy World of 5FM radio.

The list above is endless; I am trying to put across the fact that your years of employment should teach and motivate you to do something. In some cases, you were even the most dependable employee by the employer but when you leave due to retirement, voluntary separation, dismissal or whatever, you don't have to fold your hands. Take up the mantle. Strive even to bit the performance of your former employer because you know exactly what worked and what didn't work. Capitalize on what worked and steer your firm to greater heights but avoid completely what didn't work. While studying for my Bachelor of Arts degree in Economics at the University of Zambia, I worked as a part time college lecturer. Upon graduating, I joined another college as a college principal. All these colleges are long gone because of poor financial management by the owners. I started Premier College where I capitalized on what worked and have completely avoided what didn't work. Working for these defunct colleges provided me with rich insights on what it takes to run a successful college business. Remember, as I pointed out in chapter 4, the key ingredient to running a successful business is knowledge and not necessarily capital. Capital should be looked at as only a catalyst to your business but your knowledge is number one. That is why, it is always better to invest your money in the area of business where you are knowledgeable otherwise you lose out all your retirement or separation package as has happened to some people I have known in my sweet life.

FINANCIAL FAILURE
Financial failure occurs when you fail to utilize the knowledge and skills you gained as employee over the years. This forces some people to accept low paying jobs for survival. For example, if you were employed by the government as a soldier or police officer and retired after 35 years of continuous service only to get employed as security guard! Similarly, if you were employed as a banker, ending up as a bar attendant! If you were the leading vocalist in the band, like that of the Rhumba

Maestro Koffi Olomide, and then fail to lead your own band! No excuse whatsoever will suffice; the bottom line is that you have financially failed. Period!

In football circles we call that 'relegation'. You have been denoted to a lower level of football where there is less money hence professional players leave the club to join other elite clubs while they are still marketable. The coach is usually fired. Individually, fire yourself if you have failed financially.

In the Bible, there is an interesting story regarding success and failure for an individual. An account is given in the book of 2 Kings of three individuals namely Elijah, Elisha and Gehazi. For many years Elisha served Elijah as a servant and listened, observed, and thus understood what it meant to be a prophet. When Elijah was taken up to heaven in a whirlwind of fire (2 Kings 2:1), Elisha's time had come. His ministry was not as fiery and glamorous as Elijah, but he exerted a far-reaching influence. In short, he became a successful prophet. The story is different for Gehazi who served Elisha in the same capacity. The sad part of the story is the fact that Gehazi could have been doing God's work. He could have learned from Elisha. He could have been the next major prophet or perhaps a leader and teacher in the schools of the prophets. Now all he can do is speak about the good old days when he worked with the prophet. Gehazi could have been making history; now all he can do is live in the past.

There are many Gehazis in our midst. You might be one of his replicas. What you need to remember is the fact that you were born to win, but in order to be the winner you were born to be, you must plan to win. There is absolutely nothing you can do about yesterday, but the good news is that there is a great deal you can do about tomorrow. You are guaranteed a better future by doing your best today, while developing a plan of action for the tomorrows which lie ahead. Success is one thing you can't pay cash for. You have to buy it on the installment plan and make payments everyday. All you need is to combine the right attitude with specific skills; add the golden rule philosophy and a specific game plan. Now build your life on a character base and you have an excellent chance of achieving total success.

YOUR FINANCIAL FITNESS ACTION PLAN

Take a closer look at your financial journey to date, what conclusions you can draw for yourself.

QUOTES TO CONSIDER

1. George Bernard Shaw – If all economists were laid end to end, they wouldn't reach any conclusion.

2. Mohammad Ali – The man who has no imagination has no wings.

3. Robert Davies – We will find nothing in books which has no existence in ourselves.

4. Goethe – The writer only begins the book. The reader finishes it.
